A
LINE
ON
THE
BEACH

A LINE ON THE BEACH

ACTIONABLE PLAN FOR
NO TURNING BACK

DIEGO CIPION

The line on the beach
First edition: June, 2024

© 2024, Diego Cipión
All rights reserved by the author.

The publication and distribution of this work is at the author's discretion. Contact the *copyright* holders.

Printed *on* demand *Printed on demand*

Note: The copyright of this work is protected by law. Reproduction of all or part of this book, including copying, distribution, transmission or modification of the contents, without the prior written consent of the author or copyright holder, is strictly prohibited. Any violation of these rights will be prosecuted in accordance with applicable laws.

To Liannet, Vera and Lara, my wonderful lights that propel me into the cosmos.

INDEX

INTRODUCTION **13**

    A line on the beach 16

    Paralysis due to overinformation 18

    The first big lesson from all this is that less is more. 18 From marketing and with love 19

    Do not think 21

    First steps 23

    Understanding the personal situation 23

    Auditing for development and growth 25

    Defining objectives 29

HEALTH **35**

    Where to start 35

    Analysis: assess your current state of health 36

    Identify habits and possibilities for improvement 38

        Eating habits 38

        Hydration 41

Listen to your body at all times 41

Enjoyment is important 41

Resources at your disposal 43

Access to a gymnasium 43

Get to know 44

Example of a traditional gym routine 46

Example of circuit training without weights 49

Weekly menu and shopping list 51

Culinary skills 51

Summarizing 53

Some tips to keep you eating healthy 58

How to build habits 59

The 4 fundamentals 63

WORK 67

Project management 67

1. Project start 68

2. Execution 73

3. Closing 74

Marketing 75

Current status 75

Starting point 76

How to develop a generation campaign
demand and position your brand 80

Account Segmentation: 81

Market segmentation: 81

Research and identification of the ideal customer: 82

Construction of the Unique Selling Proposition (USP): 84

Identification of the Buyer's Journey: 84

Create a category: 86

Content Map Design: 86

Identification of Distribution/Creation Channels
of Demand: 87

Identification of Demand Capture Channels: 88

MONEY 91

Analysis of the current financial situation:
Preparing for the Economic Storm 95

Analysis of personal financial situation 97

Identification of areas and sources of income 101

Identification of areas and sources of income 104

Beware of false gurus and promises
of instant riches 106

Forms of corporate financing 107

Line of credit 108

Corporate loan 109

Purchase Order (PO) 110

Merchant Cash Advances 110

Hard Money 110

Inventory Advances 111

Factoring 111

Business Helper Loans 111

LOVE 115

Section 1: Analysis 115

Identifying Patterns or Traumas 118

Section 2: Resources 119

Professional advice 119

Section 3: Implementation 121

How to talk and argue without ending up shouting 122

Examples of real-life cases 123

Children. Enjoyment and education at the same time 125

Structure and order 126

Spending time, dedication and effort 129

Prioritization 130

Plan quality time 130

Self-care 130

Section 4: Some Tips 131

Impact of Social Networks 131

Conflict Management 133

Focus on Self-Esteem 134

EPILOGUE 135

INTRODUCTION

This is born out of being really tired of all the crap you find both on social media and in self-help books that are dedicated to spinning the same idea for 350 pages of relle- no. The goal of this book is to be actionable. I want to give you specific advice and a plan to follow to establish a foundation in what I consider to be the fundamental pillars in everyone's life.

I am not, nor do I plan to be a motivational, health, work or family guru. Nor am I one of those kids who post super fast videos on Instagram with a rented Lamborghini explaining lies about how to make $20,000 in a month. What I am, is a family man with a wife, a job as a marketing director and an unhealthy eagerness to learn, to want to be a better person, to give the best to my people and to be healthy long enough to enjoy them. And of course, by the way, to earn enough money to stop being a worry.

I don't have the typical personal story you find in self-help books. I am not going to tell you about a past of drugs, bankruptcy, swords against the wall, horrific parents and other dramas. Nor do I have traumatic divorces, single mothers or moments of personal enlightenment with a guru in India.

It seems that to succeed in life you have to come from broken homes and absolute trauma. No wonder then that many of these pseudo gurus are as crazy as a goat. I am a normal guy, who a few years ago emigrated to the USA from Spain and made a living starting from scratch. One can have personal traumas or defects from the beginning, one can also start the path from the starting point or a few steps ahead or behind, what becomes clear to all of us with age is that what really matters is to keep walking. We are not going to judge anyone here, but neither are we going to pat you on the back for your good or bad luck in life. This is about tools.

I am a parent with two young daughters who has often struggled with consistency when it comes to executing diets, routines or training plans. I have had my moments, my exploits, motivations and failures. I am not a robot and I struggle to be consistent. I am a human and I like to eat well, laugh and lay on the couch and do nothing. I don't claim to have a six pack, nor do I drive a Porsche to my office in a skyscraper. On the other hand in my career, I work as a marketing director in a financial institution and I have had the opportunity to do campaigns and work for very well known brands worldwide. As I have always had the opportunity to move from one job to another without too much trouble, I have never found myself between a rock and a hard place or with the urge to be an entrepreneur. It can be said that having always been a salaried employee has not put that firecracker in my ass that gives me insecurity and I have lacked that "hunger" to go out on the street, but it has always been my dream. What has happened is that, having been an emigrant, I have never had an economic cushion to take the risk and on the other hand, I have never been able to take the risk,

when I have tried I have failed. I could tell you that the reason for those failures has been not dedicating the necessary time or not having the freedom of action, but it is simply not having that urgency, not having that need and not having a consistency and a concrete plan of action. But that is going to change from now on, isn't it?

At the end of the day, when you're a wage earner, you don't have that latent fear of knowing you can pay at least a few bills. I will never say that the carrot on the donkey will make you feel satisfied, but the problem is that it takes away your hunger momentarily.

Therefore, with this book I would like to do an exercise with you to check up on yourself. If you probably read this book long after it has been written, and I am still a slightly overweight flabby guy, then it could be said that this method is not effective and you should not read any further.

As you might have guessed by now, my starting point is not that of a personal trainer who is square and has been starting chicken and broccoli all his life saying it's extremely easy. No shit! If that's all they've been doing for the past few years, it doesn't take any effort at all to do it. I want to make it clear that I am like you, and that I also had to start from scratch in this project. That I like to steal the Halloween chocolate from the girls (it's a secret between you and me, hey!) and that sometimes I go to the gym to do "cardio" and I walk at old lady speed for the whole duration of the podcast. Yes, I'm one of you, and if I can transform, then so can you because I assure you I'm nothing special.

A line on the beach

Hernán Cortés, someone loved or hated depending on who tells you the story, upon reaching the coast of Mexico did something rather contrived but which serves to illustrate what we are going to do from this point on. They reached the beach and there was a mutiny among his men because they wanted to return to their base in Cuba. After solving the rebellion, he decided to "burn the ships". He asked his subordinates to set fire to all but one of the ships - some historical sources say so, others say he swept the ships, although at the end of the day it's the same thing. Obviously I'm never going to tell you to quit your job and throw yourself off a cliff with one hand in front and one hand behind. You've probably read it somewhere, but there's no point in being ridiculous at this point in life.

What I want you to do is to make you aware that this is no longer child's play. This is not a January 1 resolution that you forget on February 1. This is a pact of honor with yourself. At the end of it all, when you are about to die, the one who is going to be reproaching yourself is going to be you. You decide.

Let's go back to Hernán Cortés, because I really want to delve into what he did next because for me that is the important thing (and what is not much on record). When they turned around and naturally saw that jungle so thick and green in front of them full of mosquitoes, natives with arrows and dangers, many were struck with fear. He drew a line on the ground and pointed to the ship that was still operational telling the mutineers something like this:

"From here to the ship, dishonor and shame, and from here to there, death and glory."

Some turned back on the ship, but the rest wrote some interesting lines in the history of mankind.

I'm not asking you to be Hernan Cortes or Steve Jobs. I want you to be someone who lives great and at the end of the day can sleep at night satisfied. Whether you are anonymous or more famous than Coca Cola, the important thing is to go to bed without guilt or, as the Spartan Lacanians used to say, "What if...."

Our personal experiences may be similar or at the antipodes, but back to the point: that is not the purpose of this book. I don't intend to evangelize on a lifestyle, I don't want you to become a vegan or a Paleo-Christian. I don't want to make you feel bad about your personal choices or question your fundamental beliefs. We are old enough. In this book I intend to give options based on several years of research after reading all kinds of texts. I want to draw a map where I put all the knowledge I have acquired and consider of value with steps to follow in order to implement them. A cocktail of varied ingredients on scattered topics that can pair well or taste like stale armpit. Only time will tell. This is an exercise, with a starting point that encompasses a holistic approach with a concrete and organized plan. No scattered information and kilometer-long theories, and for God's sake, no pointless bullshit.

Paralysis due to overinformation

Have you ever experienced information paralysis? If you are like me, you have gathered so much information from so many different sources, the starting point is blurred and you begin to have a lot of doubts about how to approach the path. In addition, you have probably seen conflicting opinions and that contributes even more to delaying your decision. On the other hand, the problem of inspirational outbursts arises. You start out with all the strength in the world and you deflate more miserably than a fart from a good plate of chickpeas.

The first big lesson
of all this is that less is more.

That's why, in many cases, the most successful entrepreneurs are not professors or scholars; their job is not to think, but to execute and learn along the way. When you learn to walk, you fall down a few times. And as cliché as this example sounds a thousand times over, we often forget it.

Since you can unlock your cell phone, you can see a hundred people explaining in detail how to make a bonsai garden or how to blow up glass. Amidst all that noise it becomes harder and harder to differentiate between what is necessary and what is a waste of time. In addition to this over-information, we find that 4.5 billion pieces of content are produced every day. And it will continue to rise because with the push of a button, you can generate content with AI.

Have you looked at Instagram today for example, can you remember at least the last 3 videos you've watched? I'm not going to talk about "mindless scrolling" but it's interesting the preoccupation with saving time and watching videos in seconds, and the amount of time we spend acquiring information that we forget in tenths of a second. I would like to daydream and think that there should be some way to censor the algorithm and not watch so many things for attention grabbing and more for concrete end goals. Sure a video of kittens or perfectly manicured hands cutting hand soap is super intriguing, but it doesn't add anything of value to your ultimate goal which is to GROW.

We need a grounding wire. There's too much impersonal bullshit.

From marketing and with love.

My approach to solving this problem comes from marketing. Treat it as if it were a new campaign or product coming to market. The situation will be analyzed with concrete tools and action plans as if it were a company launching a product. But in this case the product is you.

If you don't look nice and healthy, no one will buy you. If you don't have any projection and you smell bad, nobody will want to bring you into the house. And if you are harmful and good for nothing, what are they going to buy you for? A product has the ingredients, the manufacturing, the packaging, the sale and the distribution. So let's go ahead, let's find our own little ribbon and let's find our own market.

That's what it's all about, not about being told a bunch of bullshit for a bunch of pages like: "you have to get up at 5 in the morning" or "you have 5 seconds to make a decision". Why go to such lengths to explain simple things? Do they have to sell books? 300 pages to explain why you have to make a decision in a countdown? If it's a simple concept: let it be told quickly, we're not stupid! I have nothing against all that information, a lot of it is very useful, what I can't tolerate is the way it is presented. It's as if someone tries to explain to you with a tedious lecture and ten examples how to make a Nutella spread. It's too much of a detour to justify a $20 purchase.

As a reader, I have always missed actionable books. There are very few with a step-by-step structure to really make an effective impact in life. Many of the business books that you come across give very specific brush strokes that help you really get the point across, but none give you the real step-by-step exercise to solidify the foundation of an executable plan in all aspects of life. Also depending on what you read, you have to carve out your method and that is where coaches come in with their personal enlightenments and methods based on all this information.

On the other hand, we have the social networks where we are used to having all kinds of information explained to us in little pills. In less than 30 seconds they have explained to you the meaning of life. In a world where everything is faster and nobody stops to watch the sunsets, it is normal that this way of transmitting basic and sometimes yellowish concepts is effective. It seems real to me.

This is useful for basic concepts, but if you want to define a plan of action, you must delve a little deeper into the subject and above all give yourself time to assimilate the information.

It is normal to have doubts, inaction and, above all, to fall into anxiety and procrastination.

No to think.

Let me explain, I don't mean that everyone becomes an airhead. It's just that there are times when, like a switch, you have to be aware of when to turn on and when to turn off. I know this is stupid to some people, but I'll give you a historical example to illustrate it. Do you know when philosophy was born? In the 4th century BC. In Miletus to be exact, Asia Minor. Right next to Greece. It is the time of Thales of Miletus, Diogenes, Socrates, etc... And why at that precise moment? Some theories say that it is because for the first time in history there are many cultures that coexist and that makes human beings wonder about the meaning of life and their position with respect to the gods. It may be valid, but it is still a step ahead of my theory. For me, there is a crucial reason in this historical moment and that is that this was the first time in history in which a part of the population had food security.

When you are hungry, you only think about eating. After you eat, that's when you think about other problems. If you have food, then you are not thinking about looking for food, so you can sit and chat with your friends and become a philosopher. I know more than one that after a good barbecue they know a lot about the meaning of life, for example. And when your stomach is full and your primary needs are satisfied, that's when you start to think outside the box. It is not for nothing that at the present time in the developed countries there is the most depression. Fortunately, Maslow's primary needs such as breathing, feeding, drinking, resting and sleeping are satisfied, at least in developed countries. That is why we can only continue to think about more and more.

Let's take other examples: if there are wars, you don't stop to think: you try to survive. If there is a danger, you don't stop to find out what's going on, you probably shit or pee to lighten your load and run away.

We are still animals, but thinking animals. So in that duo we have to make decisions about when to be more or less animal. And all that is achieved with a plan. Something that tells you exactly what to do at any given moment and you don't have to question it, so you can occupy your thinking capacity on more important matters. Don't stop to question what you are going to eat today, what exercise to do, what to wear, or what time to get up. Eliminate decision making on secondary things and dedicate your gray matter to more important things like solving problems in your business, how to surprise your partner or how to make more money.

But let's not get ahead of ourselves.

> *Walker, there is no path,*
> *the path is made by*
> *walking. Antonio*
> *Machado.*

First steps

As in any business project, you have to organize the elements you have at your disposal, the time and the objectives. It is often said that all roads lead to Rome, but that is a lie. If you don't know where you want to go, there is no way you will get there.

Obviously in each person's life there are a series of specific objectives. Each person has his or her own needs and situations, but I think that if you assimilate a structure and get inertia from a basic objective, it is much easier to get up to speed to be really focused on what you really want to pursue and you yourself, after you have picked up speed, put the icing on the cake... Do we agree?

Understanding the situation personal

I believe it is appropriate to do an exercise of introspection. Obviously, each person is different and, thank God, we all have strengths and weaknesses. Precisely for that reason, it is important to be aware of what you are good at, what you want to take advantage of, exploit or eliminate.

- You should reflect on past experiences, whether they are work-related or not.

Has there been any identifiable achievement of which you are proud? What did you do to achieve it?

— It is important that you get feedback from the people you know and trust best. Maybe they see you in a way that you wouldn't even have thought of. Is there something that people who love you have always told you? For example, if they tell you that you are stubborn, nervous, strong? Do you have any emotional baggage, any complexes?

— The same as before, the first thing I recommended was to talk to a specialist to know where to start from, in this case I recommend the same. It is time to end the stigma of talking to a psychologist. It's not the 1950's, nor are you going to be pumped full of pills. You just need effective tools from a guy who is degreed and a specialist, and not some pseudo-trashy guru who has popped up on your Instagram. Watch out for that.

— You probably already know it, but take an online test of your personality type. I recommend the Myers-Bri- ggs Test (MBTI) for one of 15 personalities. Strengthsfinder (CliftonStrenghts) identifies you among 34 personal talents. There are several others, and any of them can be useful as a starting point reference. Although I recommend you not to get obsessed with it, since many of the things are assumptions without concreteness as if you were reading a horoscope. Oh, and by the way, the horoscope, don't even bother to look at it.

– See what your interests are. Usually what you are interested in is what you are naturally gifted at. If your interest is sitting on the couch looking at your cell phone, for example, you should consider exploring new experiences and taking on new challenges. You may discover skills you didn't know you possessed.

Now, put some coffee or tea on the table and go to the bathroom. Reserve your next hour for yourself without interruptions. Grab a pencil and paper (I recommend writing it down by hand for better assimilation) and put the phone on silent away from you.

Audit for development and growth.

Copy this table and answer as best you can. Don't stress about answering all the questions, if you don't know for sure, answer to the best of your ability.

Appearance	Key Questions	Space for Responses
Personal Vision	• How do I imagine myself in 1 year? • How do I imagine myself in the future in general? • What accomplishments do I want to have achieved? • How do I want to be remembered?	[Your answer here]

Personal Mission	• What motivates me every day? • What activities make me feel fulfilled? • What value do I bring, how do I Can I help?	[Your answer here]
Personal Values	• What values are most important to me? • How do these values guide my actions and decisions?	[Your answer here]
Strengths	• What are my greatest skills? • In what areas do I receive the most praise or recognition? • How can I apply my strengths to overcome challenges?	[Your answer here]
Weaknesses	• In what areas do I feel less confident? • What constructive feedback have I received? • What steps can I take to improve in these areas?	[Your answer here]
Opportunities	• What current trends could benefit my objectives? • Are there people or resources around me that I am not using? • How can I create or search for opportunities?	[Your answer here]

Threats	• What external obstacles could affect my plans? • How would my plans change in the face of unforeseen situations? • How can I prepare myself?	[Your answer here]
Objectives a Short Term	• What do I want to achieve in the coming year? • What concrete steps can I take in the short term to move toward my vision? • How can I measure my progress?	[Your answer here]
Objectives a Long Term	• What do I want to achieve in the next five years? • How do these objectives align with my overall vision and mission? • What resources will I need to achieve these objectives?	[Your answer here]

Once you have completed that table, the next step is to condense the information. Identify key elements, motivations and behaviors.

For the Vision, focus on the future and dream. Keep your language clear and concise.

For the Mission: focus on your motivations and purposes.

Let's take some examples:

- **Technology Entrepreneur with Family**
    - Personal Vision: *"To be an innovative leader in the technology field, balancing my professional career with quality time dedicated to my family, and being an example of work-life balance for others in my field.*
    - Personal Mission: *"To develop advanced technological solutions while maintaining a firm commitment to my family, prioritizing time with them and fostering an environment of mutual support and growth".*

- **Family Focused Banking Clerk**
    - Personal Vision: *"To achieve a leadership position in the banking sector, promoting ethical and responsible financial practices, and being a pillar of stability and support for my family".*
    - Personal Mission: *"To work with integrity and commitment, offering reliable financial advice and balancing my professional career with a commitment to the well-being of my family."*

For the SWOT (Strengths, Weaknesses, Opportunities, Threats) first of all be honest and realistic. Done well, it will give you self-awareness and help you identify those areas and strategic basis for defining your short- and long-term objectives.

For the C/P and L/P Objectives, focus on the field above all personal. Later there will be a strategy to do so in the professional field.

Defining objectives

As a marketing person, the first thing I'm going to ask you is: What is your objective(s)? Then let's define them. By the way, I know this start can be a bit tedious, but it is essential to ensure success. It is always necessary to do a market research, that's why this step is fundamental to know for sure all the details and define your personal strategy.

Ok, grab your pen and paper again. Hopefully it will be a different day than the previous exercise, you need to be calm and cool. Based on the C/P and L/P objectives you blurred in the previous section, answer these questions.

Aspect a Evaluate	Key Questions	Space for Responses
Past Performance Review	• What important decisions have I made in my personal life in the past? • Which of these decisions have contributed positively to my well-being and which have not? • What personal lessons have I learned learned from these experiences?	[Detailed answers]

SMART Objectives	• What are my current objectives? • Are these objectives specific, measurable, achievable, relevant and time-bound? • How can I improve or refine these objectives so that they better align with my goals? aspirations?	[List of objectives and evaluation] [List of objectives and evaluation] [List of objectives and evaluation] [List of objectives and evaluation
Key Performance Indicators (KPIs)	• What indicators do I use to measure my progress (e.g., health, emotional well-being, skill development)? • Are these indicators effective in reflecting my progress towards my objectives? • How can I adjust or change these indicators for a better evaluation?	[Description of KPIs and settings]
Alignment with the Personal Life	• How do my goals align with my family, work, social and health life? • Are there conflicts between my goals and other important aspects of my life? • What changes can I make to improve this alignment and to achieve a better balance?	[Alignment analysis and improvement plans].

Plamification of Resources	• What resources do I need to achieve my personal goals (time, funding, emotional support)? • How do I plan to acquire and manage these resources? • Is there a gap in my current resources and how can I address it?	[Resource planning and evaluation]
Continuous Review and Adaptation	• How often do I review and adjust my objectives and strategies? • How do I adapt to changes in my personal life or environment? • What actions can I take to continuously improve in the pursuit of my goals?	[Review and adaptation strategies].

Yes, I know it's too many questions. That's why I recommended a coffee before. Besides, all these questions are meant to illustrate a way and have a reason to be. If you want a meaningless question to make you think, here's one: how far do bald men wash their faces?

Once you have completed the exercises of defining your goals and answered all the relevant questions, you will have a clear and accurate understanding of where you are headed. I believe this clarity is essential for success in any area of life. Knowing your goals, your strengths, your weaknesses and the resources at your disposal allows you to chart a realistic and effective path toward your goals.

aspirations. Now there are no more half measures, but a clear path that opens up through all that thicket. You are welcome.

In this book, I have organized the approach from a structure that is perhaps a bit cliché, but tremendously effective and easy to follow: Health, Money, Work and Love. These four modules cover the fundamental aspects of life and will provide you with a comprehensive and already recognized framework.

Module 1. Health

Here, the focus is on physical and mental well-being. We will develop a plan of action in this area that will help you improve your health, diet and habits. This is an essential foundation for success in other areas of life.

Module 2. Money

This module addresses financial management and economic prosperity. You will develop skills to better manage your finances, learn about financial products and solutions. We will also analyze the pattern of the economy. This exercise will enable you to make more informed and confident money decisions.

Module 3. Work

In the work module, we apply the project management methodology to develop a structured action plan and achieve end-to-end project completion. With practical strategies and measurable objectives.

Module 4. Love

This module is about personal and emotional relationships. Here, the objective is to cultivate healthy and nurturing relationships, both romantic and platonic, which are vital for a full and balanced life.

Each of these modules includes a detailed action plan that will give you a clear starting point and guide you step by step. At the end of this book, I intend for us to not only have a deep understanding of what we want to achieve in each of these areas, but also the tools and strategies to make those dreams come true.

Remember, the key to success is action. This book is designed to not only provide you with knowledge, but also to spur you to action.

HEALTH

Where to start

Within the health of each one we must pay special attention to behaviors and current situation. Here I list what for me are the fundamental aspects in the health of each one, and therefore we will attack with a specific plan. First list the points to be treated and the reasons:

1. **Preventive care**

    Have regular medical check-ups to prevent and know what the current situation is.

2. **Maintain a healthy weight.**

    I don't want you to become an Instagram model. Nor do we want to become a "skinny" model. What we want is for everyone to be comfortable with the weight they're at without having to be fighting daily with the scale and the plate of broccoli. This is not about a month of absolute physical pain with a ridiculous diet. But about establishing a habit that makes those changes welcome.

3. **Balanced diet.**

    Understand the nutritional elements of a balanced diet. Don't starve yourself for a week by bloating on green juices, artichoke diets or ridiculous cleanses. I am going to recommend what works for me personally and you can adapt from there.

4. **Physical activity.**

    A sports routine is essential. You have to find the time. I could tell you that if there is time to watch Netflix, then there is time to train, but I don't want to go to the cliché. There has to be time for everything, so let's get organized.

5. **Adequate hydration.**

    For God's sake. Drink water.

5. **Sleep.**

    Remember the sleeping power of that high school teacher? Imagine you live with him and you have to go to bed at a reasonable hour.

Now let's go to the plan.

Analysis: evaluate your current health status .

First of all, make an appointment with your family doctor. Have a complete health examination where you will have a blood test, check-up and risk factor evaluation. You have

You should pay special attention to factors such as blood pressure, cholesterol and glucose to understand your health status and dictate the next steps and intensity.

When I came to the United States from a country where social security covered all my medical expenses, I had no idea how lucky we were not to have to pay so much money for medical care. In the U.S. it has become an abuse and, in my opinion, the problems are not usually because the doctors are or are not the ones who send you ridiculous bills or do a bad job. The problem in the U.S. is the private health insurers who inflate the price and have managed to use their position as a middleman to drive prices to ridiculous amounts. In recent years doctors are doing more work and earning less, and in turn insurance costs more and more expensive. This system stinks.

But well, enough of talking about policies because this book does not intend to dogmatize anyone but to give solutions. For the moment, the cheapest option is to use OBAMACARE. Even if you are a salaried employee with W2, you should look at this option because in the same companies the medical insurances usually inflate the prices. As for Obama-care, there are plenty of agents who can get you a license with very affordable companies and the amount you pay for your health insurance is adjusted to your income. If you happen to be self-employed, that's also your best solution, unless you have an income of, say, more than $150,000 a year, then they are not competitive. There are tricks to getting the best insurance at the best price, all you have to do is find good agents who will help you not to have to pay ridiculous amounts for a cure. So, if you are ever admitted, always ask for a detailed invoice, it's amazing the things you see.

Even so, health insurance is necessary. First you need to do your homework to know your starting point and keep track of your progress. If you are really serious about it, schedule your appointment and get the necessary check-ups knowing the efforts and measures you can take. This will be your starting point and in the long run you will feel great knowing where you have evolved from.

Identify habits and possibilities for improvement.

Eating habits.

We need to reflect on our food choices and eating patterns including meal times and preferences. For me, I traditionally get cravings after 8 p.m. With my two daughters, it is really hard to stay away from the sweets we have in the pantry. With my two daughters, it is really hard to stay away from the sweets we have in the pantry. I confess that I have often failed, and that I have learned from failure. I have seen that if I don't eat well during the day, I get hungrier than an ox at night. You know the saying about having breakfast like a king, lunch like a prince and dinner like a beggar? Well, in my case it's physically the opposite. First thing in the morning, I'm not hungry. In the evening, on the other hand, I find it hard to resist a plate of appetizing food. And of course, we all know that at night is the time to eat the least. Some people say the opposite, but if you're like me, you might want to take advantage of that.

that and try intermittent fasting. That is, not eating anything during 15 hours (from 8 pm to 1 pm).

As for the type of diet, I am going to recommend you from a "paleo" basis. This is not to say that if another option works for you that you should not try it, but as this is about giving you an actionable plan, I will give you my approach below. For example, I have tried the 100% vegetarian diet but in my case it didn't work because I didn't have enough energy and didn't feel satisfied. If it works for you, go for it! In my case and to lose weight, what has worked for me is the Keto diet, but after talking to nutritionist friends, they have told me that in the long term the consequences that this diet and others can have on health are not yet known. That is not to say that it is negative or positive for you, but the basis of the comment lies in the long term lack of knowledge as these are very new diets. What we do know is that sugar and carbohydrates are your enemies, and fats must be taken for what they are.

For all these reasons, and without wanting to get into things that I am not a specialist in, I was recommended that the best plan of action is to do a reset for a couple of months, that is to say, to adopt one of those strict correction diets for a period of two months to readjust the body and build new habits and then return to a healthy and balanced diet. That is, adopt one of those correction diets for a period of two months to readjust the body and build new habits and then return to a healthy and balanced diet, you will know what to eat, and unless you are a convulsive ignoramus, you will know exactly what foods are good for you. The truth is that after a reset it is much easier to continue with an eating plan from a healthier base.

Keep in mind that diets are difficult to maintain because they fall outside of our habits, but if you're going to shock the body with one of these extreme diets, try not to extend it too long in time. You will neither be happy nor will it be sustainable. This is not about starving yourself and sacrificing yourself for a few months, and then return to bad habits, but to change your eating style without costing you effort.

It is therefore essential that you analyze your food preferences. For example, there will always be some substitute food for chard. yuck! Explore the varieties. If an online diet you download recommends something you don't like, look at foods that may be in the same family that do the same job. The important thing is not really whether you have to differentiate between lettuce and spinach, the crucial thing is to differentiate between processed and unprocessed foods. Always giving vital importance to unprocessed foods. That is, the part on the right as you enter the supermarket and that is so expensive.

What is your eating schedule? You need to follow a consistent pattern for breakfast, lunch and dinner. Identify where you eat more or less and put a stop to it. If necessary add an extra meal to avoid major problems.

Do you eat out of necessity or excitement? I have a trick. At night, when I get the ogre hunger, I think about whether I feel like eating a chicken breast or not. If I don't want breast and instead I want chocolate, then I'm talking about emotional eating. Not for physical reasons. We have to observe and put a stop to those moments when you turn to food as a response to stress, boredom or emotions. If in the evening, you sit down to watch Netflix and you get hungry (even after you've had dinner), well.

you may want to either not sit and watch Netflix for a while to end the craving or identify what's going on and put a stop to it.

Hydration

Please don't turn into the typical freak who carries a gallon of water everywhere he goes. That seems ridiculous to me if you have easy access to drinking water. Just keep it on your radar - there are even apps that remind you to drink water! Get in the mindset that you have to drink 3 liters a day and make a life for yourself. It's not that hard. If you don't remember, you'll have to make up for it later, but don't go to bed without drinking those 3 liters.

Listen to your body at all times

Measure yourself by the energy and vitality you have. If you feel better, clearer, more focused and more active, then you are doing the right things. If, on the other hand, you feel tired, ache here and there and your belly is doing strange things, then something is not working.

Pay attention to whether or not you are hungry and what kind of hunger you have. This is the biggest hurdle and where we censor ourselves. Is it a food with saturated fats, carbohydrates, sugars or salt? Is it the only thing I can eat?

Enjoyment is important

Regarding the last point, I don't want to get caught up in evangelizing to you the same old talk about healthy eating that everyone else spouts.

Look, we already know what is good and what is bad. I'm sure you don't even need to be reminded. What you really know that you need to do is to make up your mind and be disciplined with the fact that sometimes you have to shut your mouth and other times, when it is really worth it, you have to give yourself a proper tribute. Choose the moments.

Because life has to be lived and neither you nor I want to take pictures of us showing a six-pack. It's clear that you like bread, chocolate and hamburgers, now the only thing to do is to raise awareness - I know we are no longer 1y years old and we don't have that metabolism. You're probably over 30, have some hernia and an incipient belly, so we have to pick our battles. Like cyclists. When they are young they sign up for the Tour de France, the Giro, the Tour de France and all the classics, as they get older and their legs don't climb the mountains the same way, they go to fewer competitions and end up only racing the San Sebastian classics and the occasional very select race. Apply that to parties and hangovers, for example. When you are 20 years old, there is no such thing as a hangover! At 40 something, the hangover from 3 miserable glasses of wine lasts until the following Friday. Yuck, right? With what we have been! Those were the days when we used to get up half an hour before going to bed to party. Well, not anymore, and do you know what the worst thing is? That depending on what you choose from now on will indicate whether it is uphill or downhill.

Neither Attila, nor Scipio, nor Napoleon, nor Julius Caesar raised battle in adverse conditions.

Know your body, respect it and when you decide to go out to battle, enjoy it thoroughly because at our ages it cannot be repeated frequently.

Resources at your disposal

It's time to think about what you have at hand to really achieve your goals. Do you have access to a gym or exercise equipment? Do you know how to cook and some nutrition?

Since this is about being actionable, I'm going to assume that in both cases it's yes. If this is not the case, join a gym right now and watch a Youtube video to learn how to cook a specific dish in which you may have doubts. It is not so difficult in both cases and I will not stop to give you reasons if you do not even know how to make a boiled egg. Besides, if you haven't bothered until now, it is time for you to get your act together because maybe that is one of the reasons for your failure.

Access to a gym

Plan schedules. Organize your schedule so that there is a set time and day to go. Rain or shine you have to be there. In my case that is a problem because with two little girls I have to get up super early and at night I have no energy or desire. It is a pain to get up so early in the morning, but if your case is like mine, then at night less TV and so you get the necessary 7-8 hours of sleep.

Explore the classes you like best if you are motivated by a group. There are fabulous gyms with group classes for all kinds of routines and exercises that make it super enjoyable to attend. I think at least 3 days a week you should do cardio. If in addition to

If you like one of the specific classes, take advantage of it for variety and motivation. You can also look for a group activity with friends like playing soccer, going for a run, or playing frisbee in the park. But make sure it's cardio that counts, it's no good saying that the important thing is to keep moving. It's no good to walk like an old lady unless you have an injury that prevents you from doing so and that's where you have to start. You have to sweat. If you sweat, then it's cardio, if you don't sweat, then it's a walk and doesn't count as cardio. Don't fool yourself or be fooled. It helps a lot to obviously do it with friends and if possible to have a bite with someone. The challenge should not only be with yourself, but also with someone who motivates you.

Get to know

There are 3 body types: endomorphs, ectomorphs and mesomorphs. While no one is ever 100% one of each and with age and habits can change, it could be summarized as follows:

1. Endomorphs: have slower metabolism, tendency to accumulate fat and problems to build mass. They tend not to be good with carbohydrates, they are more overweight. This is the friend who was always chubby and sweating too much. Also as we get older and change our lifestyle and eating habits, we join this group.
2. Ectomorph: Thinness, sunken chest, fast metabolism, difficulty gaining weight. They are those who are thin even if they eat a whole plate of french fries and require a lot of weight.

more calories to put on weight. In this group are the "flaqui gordos". It's not all so wonderful, is it? They are the skinny ones with thin bellies and skinny little arms, you know the ones with the beer belly?

3. Mesomorph: It's that friend of yours that you've always hated because no matter what he did he was always in shape. Privileged genetics with athletic and muscular builds that gain and lose weight easily. We all hate them, especially when they say cliché phrases like: Oh, it's so easy, it only took me a week.

Fortunately none of them is 100% one of them and as I said, depending on habits and lifestyle we can move from one to another. Of course, you have to be very clear about where you start from, and one of the 3 will be your majority.

It is essential to identify them in order to know what type of training is best for you. In simple terms, the endomorph has to do more cardio and the ectomorph more weights. The mesomorph, a balance between the two.

With this in mind, there is a way to get a routine tailored to your needs. I recommend a friend who is an instructor, or even an app or AI. Anyway, here is a specific plan that gave me good results.

You can go to a regular gym or join Crossfit, Bootcamps, Hiit, Yoga or Kick Boxing. The important thing is that you have a clear routine and set times to do it. Choose what works for you and for the love of God, do it while keeping your heart rate up.

high so you can work up a sweat. If you must, use an iWatch, FitBit or any other meter, but keep track of what you do and don't use the ever-present excuse of "I don't have time". If you don't have it, find it.

Below I put an example of a bodybuilding routine to do in any gym with a standard of equipment, but to be honest, I mix it with a gym membership in a gym that does calisthenics and circuits. Anyway, nowadays and the way the AI is, you can get a multitude of plans tailored to your needs and situation and completely free...

Example of a traditional gym routine

DAY 1. BiCEPS, TRiCEPS

CARDIO: 45 minutes.

TRiCEPS:

- Close Grip Flat Bench Press 3-4 x 8-12
- Machine Wall Raises 3 x 8-12
- Overhead high pulley extensions 7 x 8-12
- Skull Breaker 7 - 8-12

BiCEPS

- Alternating curl with dumbbells 3-4 x 8-12
- Preacher curl on machine 3 x 8-12
- Barbell curl 7 x 8-12

DAY 2:

PiERNaS

CUadRiCEPS

- Leg extension 3-4 x 8-12
- Squats 4x8-12
- Hack squats or leg press 3x8-15

FEMORaLES

- Leg bending lying down 3-4 x 10-15
- PEso Muerto with straight legs 3-4 x 10-12
- Leg bending 3-4 x 10-15

ESTiRaR.

DAY 3: aCTiVE DISCOVERy

- CaRdiO: 20 minutes relaxed.

ESTiRaR.

DAY 4: CHEST AND TRICEPS

CHEST

- Dumbbell inclined press 3-4 x 8-12
- Inclined openings (Butterfly) 3 x 8-12
- Machine press or dumbbell press 3 x 8-12
- Contracture or pulley crossover 7 x 8-12

TRICEPS:

- Close Grip Flat Bench Press 3-4 x 8-12
- Wall or machine bottoms 3 x 8-12
- Overhead high pulley extensions 7 x 8-12
- Skull breaker 7 x 8-12

DAY 5: SPAIN and twins

ESPALDA:

- Pull-ups with neutral grip 3 x failure
- Wide grip pull-ups 3 x 12
- Barbell Rowing 3 x 8-12
- Pullover 7 x 8-12

TWINS

- Standing Lift 4 x 10-12
- Seated Lift 4 x 15-20
- Lifts in press or calf machine 7 x 10-12

CARDIO: 30 minutes.

DAY 5: SHOULDER AND BICEPS

CARDIO: 30 minutes.

SHOULDER

- Seated Dumbbell Press 3 x 10-12

- Barbell or dumbbell front raises 3 x 8-12
- Lateral raises 3 x 8-12
- Lateral Lift Machine 7 x 8-12
- Rear shoulder dumbbell raises 3-4 x 12-15
- Back shoulder raises with pulley 7 x 12-15

BICEPS

- Alternating curl with dumbbells 3-4 x 8-12
- Preacher curl on machine 3 x 8-12
- Barbell curl 7 x 12-8

DAY 7: DISCOVERY

Do absolutely nothing. If God is at rest, so are you.

Example of circuit training without weights

Total duration: Approximately 30-40 minutes, including warm-up and cool-down.

Station 1: Cardio

- Warm-up: 5 minutes of light jogging or light jumping.
- Exercises:
    - Scissor jumps (30 seconds)
    - Running in place with knees elevated (30 seconds)

- Jumps with separation of legs (30 seconds)
- Rest between exercises: 10 seconds
- Rest at the end of the station: 1 minute

Station 2: Strength

- Exercises:
    - Squats with jump (30 seconds)
    - Push-ups (30 seconds)
    - Alternating lunges with jumping (30 seconds)
- Rest between exercises: 10 seconds
- Rest at the end of the station: 1 minute

Station 3: Agility

- Exercises:
    - Box jumps (30 seconds)
    - Climbers (mountain climbers) (30 seconds)
    - Lateral jump over cone (30 seconds)
- Rest between exercises: 10 seconds
- Rest at the end of the station: 1 minute

Station 4: Core (Abdominals)

- Exercises:
    - Plank with arm rotation (30 seconds)
    - Abdominal bicycles (30 seconds)
    - Leg lifts (30 seconds)
- Rest between exercises: 10 seconds
- Rest at the end of the station: 1 minute

Cooling

- 5 minutes of stretching focused on the whole body, prioritizing the areas worked.

Weekly menu and shopping list .

Culinary skills.

Explore healthy recipes and substitutes. From a specific base, it is easy to start lifting. Don't worry, I'll give you a specific plan later. Also research recipe options that suit your skills, time and budget. On Youtube there are a lot of people who teach easy step by step recipes. In my opinion, you can follow people online who explain you about diets or food, that's always good, but I recommend that if you are very fat you talk to a nutritionist to put you on a specific plan. Don't do crazy things with your body or money.

Another thing that often happens is that we see one of these onli-gurus.

ne who manages to convince you of her wonderful diet and you find yourself buying almond flour, organic black lentils and chlorophyll drops at Whole Foods at bishop's ball prices. You get your hopes up, it gets into your brain as she shows you how easy it is and as she cooks shirtless in a kitchen with clean everything, ample space and more kitchen tools than a French chef. In minutes he has managed to make the most appetizing dish ever from a mixture of raw pumpkin seeds and smoked celery with chestnuts.

Let's not fool ourselves. If you haven't done it so far, it's hard to start now. What you want is a diet that is easy, doesn't cost you your retirement money and is healthy. At least, to start with.

Starting from the premise that I don't like to go hungry and that the most important thing to avoid is to eat between meals, what I propose here is a two-step plan. The first step is to make a routine to start "cleaning" and build some habits. This doesn't mean it's the healthiest food in the world, but I put it here because it's what works for me. I started doing it for two weeks, to get used to it, and then I started with a more specific plan of higher caloric restriction to lose weight and be healthy (which is what I wanted). What you can not pretend is to make the approach to the beast and want to maintain it over time. Here we are talking about transforming a lifestyle, not to go on a diet for a few weeks and end up being as hungry as Carpanta. Therefore, the starting plan is to go little by little to build an inertia.

As for the menu, I'm not going to get all Michelin-guided or anything like that.

I'm going to propose absurd ingredients. One of the things that annoys me the most about those who teach recipes (and also DIYers, by the way) is that they start explaining how to make it easy and start bringing out tools and kitchen junk with exotic ingredients that the neighborhood supermarket wouldn't even consider. The intention with this exercise is that these are meals that you can easily make and put in a tupperware to take to work.

They are simple meals, nothing super elaborate and with the purpose of being simple and nutritious. Once you get the hang of it, you can make your own variations. Always keep in mind that by cooking at home you save money, so you kill two birds with one stone.

Summarizing

This is about adopting a healthier lifestyle through a gradual approach. The eating plan does not focus on temporary restrictions or drastic changes, but on a progressive evolution towards healthier habits that can be sustained over the long term. It is clear that if we "diet" when we stop we go back to what we were before, ergo this is about "change". This gradual change guarantees a better adaptation and minimizes the risk of relapse into old habits.

We will start with a two-week introductory phase, where the diet will progressively move towards caloric restriction (because if you are worried about what to eat, it is quite likely that you are at least somewhat plump). I base it on the principles of the Mediterranean diet, which is widely proven to be one of the healthiest in the world and also because I'm Spanish and it's the one I like.

Following the principles of the Mediterranean diet, we use exclusively extra virgin olive oil as the main source of fats, eliminating other oils and butter. Meals will be complemented with legumes such as chickpeas, lentils and quinoa, which are digested slowly and provide a prolonged feeling of satiety, along with fresh salads and vegetables such as avocado and cucumber.

During the week, we will integrate blue and white fish such as salmon, tuna and sardines up to four times, avoiding the consumption of red meats and sausages, opting instead for white meats such as chicken and turkey, and occasionally smoked pork loin. Eggs will also form an essential part of the diet, consuming three to four times a week. We will supplement these proteins with a variety of vegetables such as kimchi (not very Mediterranean, but an ultra-beneficial vegetable), broccoli, tomatoes... Desserts will consist mainly of fruits and dairy products limited to cheese and Greek yogurt. For snacks, options such as yogurt with nuts and fruit smoothies are recommended.

It is essential to avoid excessive sugar consumption, so choose foods with low sugar content or, ideally, eliminate it completely. No more Celia Cruz. This excludes sweets, ice cream and potato chips from the diet.

All of these recommendations are designed to be simple to prepare and perfect to take in tupperware to work, especially Monday through Friday, making it easy to stick to the plan even in the most demanding work routine.

Breakfast: Vary your mornings without complication

Monday to Sunday, choose between:

1. Option 1: Greek yogurt with honey, walnuts and apple pieces.
2. Option 2: Whole-wheat toast with avocado, tomato and a drizzle of olive oil.
3. Option 3: Fruit smoothie with spinach, banana, strawberries and a little oatmeal.

Food: Simple, nutritious and on-the-go

Monday:

1. Option 1: Lentil salad with roasted peppers, red onion and tuna.
2. Option 2: Quinoa with sautéed vegetables and grilled chicken pieces.
3. Option 3: Whole wheat hummus wrap, arugula, grated carrot and feta cheese cubes.

Tuesday:

1. Option 1: Greek salad with chicken breast, black olives, tomato and feta cheese.
2. Option 2: Whole wheat pasta with basil pesto, cherry tomatoes and walnuts.
3. Option 3: Vegetable soup with chickpeas and a touch of smoked paprika.

Wednesday:

1. Option 1: Brown rice bowl with grilled salmon, cate-water and cucumber.
2. Option 2: Spinach salad, orange, walnuts and turkey pieces.
3. Option 3: Omelette with spinach and sun-dried tomatoes.

Thursday:

1. Option 1: Whole wheat sandwich with turkey, low-fat cheese, lettuce and tomato.
2. Option 2: Quinoa salad with roasted beets, carrot-horia and sunflower seeds.
3. Option 3: Grilled chicken breast with steamed broccoli and sweet potato puree.

Friday:

1. Option 1: Chickpea salad with crumbled cod, green peppers and lemon dressing.
2. Option 2: Chicken fajitas with peppers, onions and guacamole, served in whole wheat tortillas.
3. Option 3: Baked salmon with a cucumber, yogurt and dill salad.

Snack (Monday to Sunday)

- Greek yogurt with a mix of fresh fruits and a handful of nuts.

Dinner (Monday to Friday)

- Monday: Egg omelet with spinach and mushrooms, accompanied by a green salad.
- Tuesday: Grilled turkey steaks with homemade kimchi and fresh salad.
- Wednesday: Grilled sardines with chickpea salad and raw vegetables.
- Thursday: Baked chicken breast with tomato and oregano, served with steamed vegetables.
- Friday: Lentil casserole with turkey chunks and a variety of vegetables.

Weekly Shopping List

- Assorted fresh fruits
- Vegetables: Spinach, broccoli, zucchini, eggplant, peppers, tomatoes
- Proteins: chicken breast, turkey fillets, salmon, canned sardines, eggs, eggs, etc.
- Legumes: Chickpeas, lentils, quinoa
- Dairy: Greek yogurt

- Whole wheat bread
- Nuts: Walnuts, almonds, walnuts, almonds
- Extra virgin olive oil

I repeat: this is an example. You can talk to a nutritionist or even use free online tools that adapt the menu to your tastes, diet, budget, time and cooking skills. I recommend you take a look, but the main thing is to find the weekly menu with recipes and shopping list. That way you have everything in order.

Some tips to keep you eating healthy.

At the beginning it's hard as hell, I'm not going to lie to you. But as I've said before, you have to keep your eyes on the end goal you set for yourself. It is very tedious to do meal planning, avoid processed foods, incorporate fruits and vegetables and on top of that eat less sugar. Here are some things to keep in mind:

- Watch out for carbohydrates and sugars! That's what really makes you fat and also causes other diseases.
- Fat is not as bad as it's made out to be. Explore other diet options such as the Keto diet or if you dare to go even harder, the Whole30. Fat is good in moderation, but don't go bingeing on bacon or I see you coming!
- Beware of mobile apps that cost you a fortune. There is a lot of free material that can help you

keep track, record your physical activity or remember dates.

- Whether you are one of those who can keep records, or one of those who have a blast and then deflate, remember that success lies in continuing, not in starting.
- Stay on plan and build habits.
- If you live with children, there is probably candy and sweets. You have to have more willpower and take advantage of the situation to educate your children to consume less sugar.

How to build habits.

You may have read books or watched online videos that tell you to get up in the morning by leaving your gym clothes at the door or to overcome doubt and inertia by counting backwards from 5 and taking action. These are great tips to keep in mind, but I think the fundamental thing **is to overcome procrastination and have discipline**.

A while back I saw a video of a guy named @jordanferrone getting into a bucket of freezing water had this illuminating quote for me:

Everyone tells you that discipline is very important. But they never want to tell you why. I will tell you why discipline is so important. It is the strongest form of self-love. It's ignoring something you want now for something better later. Discipline reveals the commitment you have to your dreams. Especially in the days you don't want. The future you, depends on your current self to keep the promises you made to yourself yesterday.

Here I tell you how to create habits, without beating around the bush and without needing 400 pages to explain it to you, but keep in mind that a habit is always created with discipline.

- **Set realistic goals.** We have already talked about this. Running starts with walking and a wall is built block by block. The clichés have already been said, now what I am telling you is that knowing what your goals are. Assuming they are: to be healthy, earn money and have a full life. Well, you have to be consistent and above all overcome procrastination.

- **Break down goals into small steps.** Introduce gradual changes lest you start training like hell and get injured and go back to zero again. Apply it to meals, work or training. Little by little. For example, the routine that I have put above is for when you already have a run, do not put yourself in animal plan to do 100% that you will end up in a wheelchair. Step by step, don't be a brute, we all have had the typical one week start and then we deflate like a balloon.

- **Be understanding of yourself.** Another important thing is to be aware that you will be in pain at some point and you will probably be in a bad mood about everything around you. Especially from the second week onwards. Notify to those around you that you are going to be a pain in the ass for a few days or else bite your tongue.

- **Follow-up and records**. It seems silly, but seeing the evolution feels super good, so not everything is suffering at the beginning.

- **Find activities that you enjoy**. By this I don't mean going to the bar, but activities that satisfy you in body and soul. If you enjoy what you do, you're more likely to do it in the long run. For example, I'll never understand pickleball, but if you love it and you sweat, go ahead my friend, give it your all!

- **Find friends or mentors.** We are social animals, so better alone than in bad company. If you have another friend who is as fat as you are, motivate yourself with him or her so at least you have someone to give you consistency. For what it's worth, what has worked best for me is to get together with people who are already good at it. If it's about going to the gym, it's better to go with a friend who already has the habit, not for two people who have never done it to have to build it from scratch. As the saying goes: Tell me who you hang out with and I'll tell you who you are. Another option is to do it with your partner so that you have a common goal and there are no problems of romanticism or that "we don't spend enough time together".

- **Change the perspective.** Instead of looking at the short term

    or something that you have to do for a while to lose weight

or get in shape, consider it a change of lifestyle.
life. Shift your focus and think about whether you are actually

The reason for this is precisely because there was something wrong in the first place.

- **Celebrate your triumphs**. That is very important. But don't start celebrating on Friday and finish celebrating on Sunday, because we all know each other... Make them healthy rewards and aligned with your health goals.

- **Stress**. If you told me 20 years ago that you have to meditate I would laugh that person in the face. What I have learned over time is that there are times when it is necessary to stop. Quiet the noise in your head and breathe.

- **Flexibility and forgiveness**. We all make mistakes. Don't be mortified if you screw up. Of course, don't go off the menu plan, we are not Saint Teresa of Jesus to lose at all times. You know the difference between a slip and a skid.

- **Visualize your goals**. Think about how you're going to feel when you achieve it and how good you're going to feel. It's super motivational to see yourself in that moment, but be careful, don't obsess about it.

- **Make it pleasant.** If you've tried it for a while and it's still horrendous, find another way. There are plenty of healthy options out there, maybe you need to do a little more research or try new things. Who knows, maybe you like pilates or airsoft and didn't even know it existed. This is not about suffering to be happy and healthy, it's about enjoying life to the fullest by adapting your lifestyle.

The 4 fundamental

We have already talked about habits and how to build them. We have established that our main enemy is procrastination and that the tool against it is discipline.

Now I am going to give the weapons to be very clear about how to act and how to start taking steps in the right direction.

Beyond explaining the reasons why procrastination appears, what is clear is that we all have it. There is always a first impulse that prefers inaction, whether it is because you are warm in bed or because it is too cold in the street to go for a run, what is clear is that your body will always prefer comfort to sacrifice. What your body doesn't know is that this is a short term reward and in the long term it is almost always counterproductive. But I'm not going to dwell on this. There are plenty of books that explain the scientific reasons and the purpose of this book is to give you tools and less to dig into the whys and wherefores of a given subject and give theorems in endless pages.

How do you end that first impulse? By matching that impulse with an opposing force. And above all, without stopping to think about it too much.

There is the Mel Robbins method of the countdown from 5 down in which without giving you time to rethink it, you have to activate as soon as the countdown is over. And so, like a rocket, you get out of bed or start what you were having such a hard time starting. It's like putting a firecracker up your ass and shooting off. But the ultimate goal is what we said at the beginning of the book: NOT THINKING.

Another way is to use neurolinguistic programming. If you need to focus because you have a lot on your mind, a quick and effective method is to do something that almost all of us have been doing since we were kids. Remember that moment when you gawk at a fixed, still point? In Spain we call it "estar embelesado" or "estar en Babia". It is almost like a catatonic state in which it even seems like meditation with your eyes open. If what you need is to (figuratively, don't be a bad thinker) hit the reset button to start something properly focused, you must force that situation. Stand in a comfortable place and look for a fixed point in the middle distance. Look at it carefully for a minute and concentrate only on that. After this exercise, you will have the calm and focus to start what you were postponing.

Apart from the techniques, each coach will have his or her magic formula. You can try several of them and in the end they all come to the same thing. The bare- mo goes from a new age guy to a wolf of wall street, which would be like hot and cold. There is so much choice and so many charlatans, that you find yourself one day paying a fortune for an individual who tells you that you have to get up at 5 am and do 100 sit-ups or another who recommends eating vegan and Captain Tsubasa yoga. And well, anything in between those two extremes.

You may also think, what a hypocrite the guy is giving life lessons and criticizing others like him. Probably. But I would like to think that if you have come to this part of the book it is probably because you have found valuable information so far. That's what it's all about. To compile what in my personal opinion has been of value to me.

It works for me, it puts everything in order and saves you a lot of time (and pages) of junk.

And speaking of coaches, I'm going to say a cliché: if an elite athlete, who is one of the best in the world in his specialty, always has a coach, why shouldn't you take advantage of it? Of course, be careful who you choose, because every coach has a different mentality and it's not the same to play defensively as to attack. Another option are mentors and friends with the same interests, in both cases equally or more necessary than coaches because they are free.

Without wishing to digress, I wanted to make this introductory aside because for me, having clarity is synonymous with not questioning your decisions and knowing for sure what to do at any given moment without questioning it. To do this, I recommend doing the following every morning and every day. I recommend you to do it for the next 3 months to build a habit: you will not regret it.

1. **Exercise**.

    Do something that will get you out of the mental fog and provide you with

    clarity of mind.

2. **Meditation**.

    I'm not telling you to go kumbaya, I'm just saying that for a few minutes get away from the noise and take a moment for yourself. Take the opportunity to give thanks for the good things you have in life.

3. **Purpose**.

    Define what you are going to achieve in the day. Have a clear objective and organize your day mentally.

4. **Study**.

    Learn something. Listen to a podcast, read the newspaper, whatever interests you but not for too long, you don't have to spend your day at it.

These are the 4 activities I recommend doing every morning to boost your creativity, mental clarity and productivity. Plus, I assure you that they will put you in a good mood and make you feel fulfilled.

Now all that's left is the easiest thing of all. Getting started.

WORK

As you may know, most of my work experience is in private enterprise. In this book I intend to do an effective project management exercise. Just as in a company, you could create a product or service and then launch it to the market, in this book we intend to do exactly the same but with our life. If there have been so many professionals developing methods to bring sometimes impossible projects to the market, engineers who have developed unthinkable products or architects who have thought of wonderful buildings using empirical and effective methods, why not you, my friend, would you use the same approach with your lifestyle?

Management of projects

If I were an engineer or mathematician, possibly the angle with which we would attack this chapter would be different, but as you know, I am a marketing professional working in private enterprise, so I will list step by step how to manage a project from start to finish with the necessary phases for you to start implementing them, and from there I will develop the tactics that I consider most effective to have an effective productivity.

Roughly speaking, this is the structure when a project is planned in a company:

The fundamental thing is to have a concrete objective. Then allocate the time and resources at your disposal, specify the phases of implementation, execution, follow up and analysis of results.

So, whatever tool you find online to keep track, or if there is no possibility, a pen and paper, here is the basic structure and some tips.

As for the speed of implementation, it will depend on the specific objective, but I recommend doing it in 12-week cycles. Why? Because it is 3 months and after that you will have already built the habit. In addition, having a clear start and end, you will be able to organize yourself in time and instead of doing it year by year, reducing the time creates urgency and focus. It is a quarter or as the Americans say, a quarter of the year. In this case, and if you like to delve into a particular method, I recommend reading the book "12 week year" by Brian P. Moran and Michael Lennington. In that case, it is one of the few books I have found that has a specific and actionable method in terms of productivity. We will use it as a reference.

1. Project start

Identification of the goal, need or opportunity.

Clear and specific goals must be established. Goals should be achievable, realistic and measurable. If they cannot be achieved in 3 months, then they should be segmented into phases that can be feasible.

You need to understand and analyze well the reason why you are starting the project and there can't be too many or you will get saturated.

Project planning.

Development of the project plan:

You have to establish a detailed planning and that means that the general goals established at the beginning of the project are broken down into specific actions week by week. Maybe at the beginning it is a little difficult to see the concrete objective, but if you break it down into specific and small goals then it is more feasible.

For example:

Goal 1: Lose 10 kilos (20 pounds)

Week 1-2: Establishing Fundamentals

- Start moderate cardiovascular training: 30 minutes, 3 times a week.
- Implement a balanced diet, with a daily intake of 1800 calories.
- Drink 2 liters of water a day.

Week 3-5: Building Healthy Habits

- Increase the duration of cardiovascular training to 45 minutes, 4 times per week.

- Introduce resistance training: 2 sessions of light weights per week.
- Maintain a balanced diet and caloric intake.
- Increase hydration to 2.5 liters of water per day.

Week 7-y: Training Intensification

- Add a weekly high-intensity interval training (HIIT) session.
- Continue resistance training.
- Evaluate and adjust the diet according to weight loss and energy needs.
- Maintain hydration at 2.5 liters of water per day.

Week 10-12: Focus on Final Weight Loss

- Increase the duration of cardiovascular training to 50 minutes, 5 times per week.
- Intensify resistance training.
- Re-evaluate and adjust the diet according to the final objectives.
- Ensure hydration with 3 liters of water per day.

Objective 2: Generate leads for your company

Week 1-2: Definition of Objectives and Audience

- Establish specific and measurable objectives
- Clearly identify the target audience

- Align objectives with audience expectations.
- To deepen in the investigation of competition
- Analyzing market trends and emerging opportunities
- Refine the initial strategy with information gathered

Week 3-4: Integral Strategy Development

- Configuration of Tools and Platforms
- Content Creation and Distribution
- Planning of Advertising Campaigns
- Execution of Advertising Campaigns

Week 5-8: Implementation and Continuous Refinement

- Configuration of Tools and Platforms
- Content Creation and Distribution

Week y-10: Advertising Campaigns

- Planning of Advertising Campaigns
- Execution of Advertising Campaigns

Week 11-12: Follow-up, Adjustments and Final Evaluation

- Immediate Monitoring and Adjustments
- Final Analysis and Future Planning

I recommend you to use Chat GPT to at least put the first one in.

stone in this plan. From there you adjust to your specific needs, but rather than be dealing with the dilemma of the blank sheet of paper, let the IA take the first stroke and from there you adjust.

It is very important that you continuously measure progress. This means that every day you take care of assigning a specific score. The important thing is that you achieve at least 80% of the weekly objectives set.

Risk identification.

Where can the potential screw-up be? We are all aware of our limitations and if there are any birthdays, relevant dates or risks to consider. You have to be prepared for those eventualities and develop a strategy to prevent and mitigate them. You also have to be convinced and have strategies to maintain a positive mindset and resilience to keep the momentum going or get on track.

Resources.

In principle, you are the protagonist, but you may need a personal coach or someone you trust who can help you with the successful execution of the plan. The most important thing is that he or she can help you foster that determination to achieve the proposed challenge. Whether it's to help you walk at first to jog later, or to have someone to be accountable to. I mean: that friend with whom you bet $200 that in 3 months you will be 20 pounds thinner, or that other friend who is passionate about sports and has always invited to go with him until you finally accept his proposal and start training together.

2. Execution

Start. Without looking back and taking into account what we have already talked about procrastination, habits, etc... You have a plan and you are going to get it done.

The only thing you have to do is to be constant and obtain at least an 80% success rate in the implementation. The goal is clear and you know that there are only 3 months in which at the beginning it will be difficult but once implemented, it will be a piece of cake.

Discipline and focus are essential. But not everything is going to be suffering during this process. You must also make room to celebrate your intermediate achievements such as cheat meals or buying something you crave. It is important to be clear that this is not about doing it at all costs, because you will end up hating it, what we are looking for is to change a lifestyle and above all to have a guide and structure to achieve specific goals. We are not robots and the process should not be a suffering. If sometimes it is necessary to slow down the pace, then it is evaluated and a strategic change is made, but we must always keep in mind that we seek to maximize effectiveness.

Monitoring, control and celebration.

If you see steady progress and consistency it will be much easier to get the motivation to achieve your goal. If someday failures, you will know that you have to make up for lost space. When

achieve some intermediate goal, give yourself a treat.

3. Closing

One of the most beautiful feelings is when you have achieved a difficult goal. Not only on a social level for your friends and family, but on a personal level with the feeling of pride, growth and self-confidence it gives. When you start and finish a project in a successful way, you get the feeling that life is moving forward and you are not stagnant.

Also, if you have set out to achieve a goal and you have done your best to achieve your goal, but have not achieved it 100%, it is also positive because you are probably in a better situation than when you started. You will have learned or earned more money than if you had not tried.

For example, if you set out to have a million dollars a year from now and you could do everything you could, would you make it? Who knows? You probably would, but you might not have reached that amount. What I am sure of is that you will probably have more money than if you had not tried or set that particular goal.

Evaluation and reflection

After the celebration of the objective achieved or the results, it is time to let the waters calm down and analyze the lessons learned.

and, if possible, document the knowledge acquired. Secure-mind after this step. Have already in mind new future projects.

Marketing

Before I begin this section, I want to make it clear that the objective of this book is to be effective, so I will choose to be specific. This section deserves special respect and love because I am passionate about my career and my work. However, I prefer not to go into too much detail because it would be enough for another book and the objective always deserves special respect. The exercise I will do next is to paint for you the current situation of the marketing world and its evolution and how to define an effective plan.

Current situation.

We must start from the initial point that everyone will have a forged marketing opinion. Whether they know it or not, most people are familiar with social media or have spoken to a brother-in-law who has dogmatized them on a specific tactic. While they may be partially right, you often encounter biased and uninformed opinions on marketing-related topics. It is not uncommon to hear phrases like: "what you need is a good website", "social media is everything in this world", "I've put $100 on Facebook and got nothing", "word of mouth is best" or "Google stole $200 from me because I placed an ad and it ran and I don't know how to remove it". Sound familiar?

The fact that everybody has social networks also implies

that many of them also think they know all the secrets and what works. Sometimes, I wish I was a quantum physicist or a space engineer so I would know that in a barbecue conversation the typical neighbor doesn't come over to discuss string theory. In marketing, no matter how professional or advanced you are, everyone is going to have an opinion or expertise and that's the beauty of it. No matter how little you know as a starting point, I assure you that you are not starting from scratch. The only thing you have to be clear about is that you just need to get organized and, as we have already seen, have a plan.

Starting point

I'm going to focus on online marketing. It's funny that depending on the videos or podcasts that people have listened to, they come to you with the most disparate proposals. Some people think that Google advertising is the best, or that using influencers is the secret, but I recommend that you don't let yourself be so easily convinced and take a step back and look at everything from a strategic point of view. In marketing, there are two parts, strategy and tactics. One cannot live without the other.

You have to analyze the troops you have and go into battle with the best possible organization. It is not the same to go to war with 1000 infantry soldiers, than to go with 500 infantry, 300 artillery, 50 airplanes and 50 drones. It is necessary to have very clear which are the troops that can be available and to organize them to have the best possible effect. For example, in the world of advertising agencies in the United States, it is not uncommon to come across typical examples such as those that propose to spend

What's the point of having a perfect website if no one is going to go there!

Then there are others that have an exceptional logo and the website cannot be found, or those that have spent millions on product development and have no social profiles.

Marketing must encompass the most effective tactics possible.

One of the problems we marketers face is seeing pseudo online gurus who take a picture of themselves next to a rented Maserati and explain that they have made 3 million and teach you everything for free or with a $200 course. Do you really think that if that guy has made 3 million with affiliate marketing in the last year he would be wasting his time selling a course for that price? Does the expression "Fake it until you make it" ring a bell?

I do not question the methods of some to get rich quick and there are probably a good number of them who have achieved it, but we must also be aware that it takes much more sacrifice and knowledge to do things right and probably you are already late and the sector in which they are operating and have their credibility and leverage is possibly saturated.

Moreover, all this is constantly evolving. A few years ago it was community managers, then influencers, then dropshipping, cold email, funnels, affiliate marketing, etc... They are all fads, and they are becoming increasingly saturated.

Few things have changed since the time when theater in Roman times began to be popular. When a tragedy was performed, the gods - whoever they were - had to be present: today we might call them influencers. Often, because they had to compete for public investment subsidies, saboteurs would go to the performances of rival companies to boo the show so that the audience would leave and thus expose actors who were often slaves and lived in semi-indigence.

Imagine yourself in a forum, trying to watch a play squeezed in between the screaming, fighting and spitting crowd. Representatives of other types of entertainment, such as gladiator fights or malabarists, try to take the audience away from them in the middle of the play. How? By shouting without any hushed tones among the actors' outrageous speeches, who, by the way, were not wearing a microphone because it had obviously not yet been invented. And in the face of all that noise, I am trying to see a play by Terence, who could be the Spielberg of the time, but who surely needs attention.

Now open your profile on social networks and you will see the religious post of the sanctimonious friend, the influencer showing her breakfast, the vegan guru mixing a cleaner made with vinegar, the memes in the DM of your partner and the thousand times retouched photograph of a friend with more operations than the Persian Gulf.

From time immemorial and among all the noise, there is always someone trying to tell us a story. There is visual and sound noise. Do the exercise right now: look up wherever you are and count all the marks you see with the naked eye. Those who send

THE LINE ON THE BEACH

The message has means at their disposal: cell phones, Internet, television, radio, billboards, social networks.... And the receivers of course avoid these messages as they avoid fire. It is becoming more and more complicated to really reach people and that is because often the person sending the message does not even believe what he or she is saying. We are at a point of oversaturation in which messages must be short with a hook in the first 4 seconds, and on top of that, memorable.

Have you opened Instagram today? Tell me a single video you remember. If you remember more than two, you deserve a prize. It's amazing how attention-grabbing and short-lived it is in our heads.

On the other hand, we have the evolution of platforms. Until a few years ago you could invest an affordable amount of money in advertising on Google and Meta (Facebook) and get potential customers. You just had to create a good sales funnel where the potential customer would click on the ad, get to a landing page and from there be accessible to a sales call. But after Covid, more and more companies are investing more and more money, driving up the cost per click and the keyword value. So you have to resort to much more specialized tactics where your budget is easily stretched.

The clear pattern is that there is an evolution in consumer behavior and that is that people are no longer inclined to give information and that they reject sales funnels. In recent years we see how, and I include myself among them, we want to discover the products or services on our own. If possible for free and taking advantage of the vast amount of information that can be found online and if possible, for free.

try before you buy. We are saturated with seeing the same crap over and over again and also that in too many occasions it doesn't really go in depth leaving a good hook at the beginning and no depth in what was promised. We don't want to be inundated with offers we don't want from people we don't know and we don't want to see newsletters with redundant information. As for blogs, really? We hardly consult blogs because
how can we look for information about something we don't know?

The consumer has evolved in the ability to make buying decisions and will continue to do so. This approach will allow you to identify opportunities with buyers who have recognized their needs, have a comprehensive knowledge of your company (including prices, values, methodology, advantages and equipment), are an active part of the purchase decision whether we are talking about a company, family or individual, and are at the right time to make the purchase. The result of this strategic approach is clear: the generation of opportunities that convert faster, effectively transforming leads into customers.

How to build a campaign
to generate demand and position your brand.

Understanding how customers make decisions is essential to designing an effective marketing strategy. Here's a crash course in marketing that would have come in handy during my undergrad and saved me at least two years of filler. Follow these steps in the following order and go deeper with information at line, here you have the basic guidelines. Also if you have specific questions, you can contact me on my social networks and I will clarify doubts or develop in depth.

Account Segmentation:

In order to optimize our commercial strategies, make a detailed list of segmented customers based on key criteria. This segmentation will include variables such as the industry they belong to, their size, the revenue they generate, the projects or products they have acquired, their strategic position and their long-term value (LTV). If it turns out you don't have clients yet, look on LinkedIn, ask friends in the industry or, as a last resort, go cold door. You need information.

This initial step will allow us to gain an in-depth understanding of the diversity of our customer base and, by analyzing the segments that significantly impact revenue, we will identify essential patterns and relationships. Through this information, we will delineate the market segments in which we should build the Ideal Customer Profile (ICP), providing strategic guidance to adapt our future business strategies and continuously improve our business operations.

Market Segmentation:

With the data previously collected, it is imperative to identify the most attractive market segments in order to maximize Return on Investment (ROI). This strategic process consi-

We will look at key criteria, such as the competition in each segment, market size, life cycle, monetization capacity per customer, growth potential, customer creditworthiness, potential virality, our expertise in the segment, accessibility to the decision-maker and overall profitability. By analyzing these aspects, we will be able to direct our efforts toward the segments that offer the best opportunities to achieve maximum financial impact and optimize our commercial operations.

Research and identification of the ideal customer:

To maximize the effectiveness of our commercial strategies, it is essential to develop an Ideal Customer Profile (ICP) for each market segment. Given the diversity of needs and motivations of each segment, the creation of individual ICPs becomes crucial to tailor our product or service offerings precisely. In the ICP development process, we focus especially on our "best" customers, those to whom we bring substantial value and who obviously provide us with the highest profitability. This approach is justified by considering that our best customers are those we benefit the most. The lookalike strategy will allow us to replicate the profile of these valuable customers. The resulting PCI will be used to specialize and convert more, customize our strategies, select the right channels and establish criteria to define a Qualified Lead Customer (MQL). In addition to creating PCI by segment, it will be imperative to identify all the various stakeholders within the decision-making process. If we are talking about a company, it is not

So does the accountant who needs the software and convinces his boss to give him the money to buy it. One discovers us and the other approves of us. Another example would be a food processor that the wife wants to buy and the husband who is convinced because it will produce delicious croquettes. Each of these people has a role and a behavior.

In order to obtain a more detailed view of our customers' experience and to make progress in continuous improvement, it is essential to ask them questions. These conversations will provide us with key information by answering essential questions, such as:

— What are the most valuable aspects that stand out when interacting with us?
— How does our offer impact your life?
— What elements influence their decision making when they opt for our products or services?
— Are there specific areas that we could refine?
— What are the particular challenges that our solutions successfully solve?
— What motivates customers' active search for our solutions and where have they looked?

By getting answers to these questions, we will be in an optimal position to build a Unique Selling Proposition (USP), perfect our web communication, content and emails, refine our sales pitch and develop customized content strategies that align with the needs of our audience.

Construction of the Unique Selling Proposition (USP):

Designing the Unique Selling Proposition (USP) is getting to the heart of the customer's choice. Why do they choose us? This key question encapsulates the essence of our connection with those who trust us. Careful design of the USP is not just a strategy, it is the key to forging a category of our own and, consequently, cultivating the much sought-after Brand Relevance.

How do we achieve this? We extract the essence directly from conversations with our clients, where their goals and problems emerge and the value they seek is revealed.

In the delicate art of designing the USP, we not only articulate what we offer, but build a narrative that resonates with the true essence of our value.

Remember that human beings have evolved based on telling stories around a fire. We just need to know what kind of story they will remember.

It is an invitation to explore not only what we sell, but why every customer chooses us as their preferred partner. USP is not just a message; it's a promise we deliver on every interaction, every solution and every challenge we help them overcome.

Identification of the Buyer's Journey:

The key to selling effectively lies in adapting to the way your buyers interact. Surprisingly, the y7% of the market is not at the time of purchase, but in a learning phase.

The Buyer's Journey comprises three crucial stages in a consumer's decision-making process. These stages are:

- Awareness: In this phase, the buyer identifies that he has a problem or a need. Here, he seeks information to understand and clearly define what his challenge is. The main objective is to create awareness of the problem and begin to explore possible solutions.

- Consideration: Once the buyer is aware of his problem, he enters the consideration phase. Here, he explores different options and available solutions. He compares characteristics, advantages and disadvantages of the alternatives. The objective at this stage is to evaluate which solution best meets their specific needs. They will first try to work it out for themselves with the information they have at hand. If something more in-depth is required, other solutions will probably be considered.

- Decision (Decision): In the final phase, the buyer has researched and narrowed down his options. Now, he or she makes the purchase decision. At this stage, it is crucial to provide information that reinforces the buyer's choice, such as testimonials, warranties or product demonstrations. The ultimate goal is to convert the potential buyer into a satisfied customer.

Create a category:

Guided by this Unique Point of View, we orient all our content, building a category where we stand as undeniable leaders. This strategy allows us to stand out and be recognized in a saturated market.

This step is fundamental. The category YOU INVENT.

To captivate our audience and stand out as leaders, it is essential to forge our own category. This involves:

- Discover Differences with the USP: Identify what sets us apart through our Unique Selling Proposition.
- Defining the Unique Value Proposition: Each interaction should reflect our unique value to customers.
- Formulate the Unique Point of View: Distill our beliefs into a unique perspective that positions us as leaders in the category.

Content Map Design:

The main objective is to make yourself known as the OWNER of your category and create a relationship with your audience. You should always give valuable information. If you are an expert you must go into detail on the topic. All channels are already saturated with information obtained with GPT Chat. IA goes so far, you must really dig deep into whatever you define as your specialty or category.

When it comes to issues, you must first find out what the

people are interested in listening and will probably have more resonance. You can ask on your social networks, on specialized websites (Quora, answerthepublic.com,...) or attend related events and fairs.

This step involves creating an editorial calendar with a balanced mix of content that demonstrates your expertise, engages your audience and presents your products or services in an engaging way. From selecting topics to periodically reviewing the plan and creating weekly pillars, each step is designed to ensure that your content resonates with your audience and contributes to the overall success of your marketing strategy.

Channel Identification
Distribution/Demand Creation:

In the demand generation strategy, content distribution becomes an art, where format and background play crucial roles. To accelerate this process, the possibility of using Paid Ads arises, but the key question arises: what type of campaign to choose? Combining demand generation with Account-Ba- sed Marketing (ABM) adds a level of personalization. Here, content strategies are specifically targeted, with precise steps to follow. From the creation of an Ideal Customer Profile (ICP) to the identification of distribution channels.

Every step must be planned. For sales, proactive engagement and identification of intentionality lead the way, culminating in a call to action when appropriate. The end goal is clear: to establish and cultivate a strong relationship with the audience.

Identification of Demand Capture Channels:

Identifying intentionality is a crucial step in the process, and to do so, it is essential to discern what events we consider to be signs of intentionality. Some key examples include events that could trigger a buying process, such as job changes, promotions, mentions in the press, interactions on your profile or with your content, among others. Traffic tracking tools on your website are often useful. Exploring sites with high purchase intent, such as UpWork, if it is B2B use Linkedin, or use Deep Social will give you credibility and help you position yourself as a leader in your industry.

Remember, the goal is not only to convert the sale, but to evangelize. You will probably have to interact several times with a potential customer until they are at the buying stage.

You can only convert the lead by providing valuable information and a positive experience.

Measure your results, assess content and its effectiveness

Finally, as with everything proposed above, you should analyze what you have achieved so far.

You have to consider that this is a longer term play. Give yourself at least 5 months to get quality results. Remember, you're not going into the field to hunt, you've become a farmer and you're waiting for the harvest. The metrics presented here are not focused on simply evaluating the strategy of

Demand Generation, but in understanding whether the content connects with the audience. From sales conversations to inbound lead generation, evaluated qualitatively, an effective impact is sought. The inclusion of media invitations and engagement with specific accounts is not only measured by overall reach, but by the certainty that the content reaches the right audience, whether in the context of Account-Based Marketing (ABM) or not. This approach beyond traditional metrics underscores the importance of authentic connection with the audience and the relevance of content at each stage of the funnel.

This is the only way to build a strategy with a firm foundation and not constantly depend on investing millions of dollars in advertising, creating resonance, brand value and above all a positive experience.

And we all know that what we remember is the experience, not the features or the price.

MONEY

Talking about money can indeed be a complex and, for some, even uncomfortable topic. Sometimes in a couple it is a thorny subject that many avoid. But the truth is that this topic permeates all aspects of our lives, affecting not only our ability to meet basic needs but also our ability to achieve those dreams and goals we set for ourselves. They say money doesn't bring happiness, but go ask those who live under a bridge, have crippling debt or are worried about making ends meet. Money doesn't bring happiness, but it definitely helps. The secret is to achieve that balance where money is not a burden, because it is clear that it will always be a worry. Accepting this reality is the first step in unraveling the financial enigma that so intrigues and sometimes overwhelms us.

As a parent and an immigrant, I deeply understand the need for continuous improvement, not only economically, but in all spheres of life. Curiosity, that quality that I try so hard to instill in my daughters, is also the reason why I often make the effort to try to learn about financial products and not about Vinicius' latest goal. Yes, when you're sitting on the toilet it's more fun to read about the soccer game than the about the real estate crisis, but sometimes you have to make the effort and choose the moments. In a way it is not only curiosity, but also the first initial discipline that paves the way for it to become interesting later on. It's like that book that you started to read that has 100 pages of real roll and cost you a lot, but then are necessary to read the remaining y00 pages in a couple of sleepless nights and as the boy in the movie "Neverending story". It is that same curiosity that leads me to question, research and ultimately understand that financial management is much more than abstract meaningless numbers on a spreadsheet; it is the art of making informed decisions that resonate with our values and long-term goals. At the end of the day, it is strategy and foresight.

In this sense, the money section of this book is not intended to be simply a compendium of financial tips and strategies because I am not a CFO. Rather, it is meant to be an invitation to reflect on our relationship with money, to understand how our beliefs, emotions and personal situations influence our financial decisions, and to recognize that, while the road to financial stability and prosperity can be full of challenges, it is also full of opportunities to learn and grow.

Today's dynamic and sometimes unpredictable economy requires us to be more attentive than ever to how we manage our money. There is always a crisis looming. Inflation, labor market fluctuations, financial market volatility, among other factors, can seem like insurmountable obstacles. However, with the right strategy and a mindset open to learning, it is possible not only to survive but to thrive.

Throughout this section, we explore together how to set realistic financial goals, how to create and maintain a budget that reflects our priorities, how to save and invest wisely, and how to protect our assets and financial stability in the face of potential adversity. We will also address the importance of financial education for ourselves and future generations, because understanding money is, in essence, understanding how to empower our lives. Some time ago I read in Ayn Rand's "Atlas Shrugged" a monologue by one of the characters named Francisco d'Anconia in which he offers a passionate and philosophical defense of money in a speech that has become one of the most memorable moments of the novel. D'Anconia challenges the common perception of money as the root of all evil and argues instead that money is a medium of exchange that represents human labor and creativity. He argues that those who despise money do so because they misunderstand its true nature and function. He criticizes those who condemn money and yet are the first to demand, pointing to hypocrisy in resenting those who have earned their wealth through effort and innovation. Money, according to D'Anconia, does not buy happiness, but it provides the means to achieve the values that make happiness possible. D'Anconia's speech is a call to recognize and respect the effort, integrity and ability of those who create wealth, and to reject notions that money is obtained through fraud or exploitation.

Effective financial management begins with understanding basic money principles and expands into implementing strategies that align with our personal goals and aspirations.

nal. From setting a realistic budget that reflects our values, to making informed investment decisions that enhance our long-term wealth, each step we take brings us closer to financial freedom.

In this section, we will confront myths and misunderstandings. I hope that after reading this chapter and with each myth debunked, our relationship with money will be strengthened, allowing us to see it for what it really is: a resource that, when used well, can expand our opportunities and improve our quality of life.

However, money management also requires an honest introspection about our attitudes and emotions toward money. Recognizing and overcoming fears or limiting beliefs that prevent us from achieving financial fulfillment is an essential part of this process. In doing so, we will not only transform our financial health, but also the way we perceive the value of work, effort and reward.

This journey will also lead us to explore the art of investment, not only as a way to increase our wealth, but also as a means to contribute to the development of companies and projects that share our ideals and vision of the world. We will learn to discern among the various investment options, evaluating risks and benefits, always with the objective of making decisions that are in line with our ethical and financial principles.

In my opinion, one fundamental thing must be clear: the ultimate goal is not simply to accumulate wealth, but to build a full and meaningful life. If you intend to become rich like those instagrammers who are ridiculous spenders, maybe this is not your section. I think that if you have enough money to go around, you don't deserve to have it or it will last very little. I think it is more satisfying on a human and personal level to donate it to people who do need it instead of having ridiculous parties with tattooed tits and bottles of Don Perignon on yachts, but to each his own with his life decisions. In my opinion, it is much more satisfying to have peace of mind knowing that you have contributed something good to society than to give away money to the wallets of interested friends or silicone seekers. But as the saying goes: everyone spends money the way they want.

Analysis of the Current Financial Situation: Preparing for the Economic Storm

In these times of constant economic fluctuation, the need to immerse ourselves in a deep and comprehensive analysis of our financial situation could not be more critical. The word "crisis" resonates strongly, prompting serious reflection on the instability of the current economic scenario. We face remarkable challenges, driven by rising inflation and relentlessly escalating interest rates, challenges that demand our meticulous attention and decisive action. They say that it is in times of crisis that wealth is created, so it is necessary to be on the lookout and to jump in and be prepared for opportunities. For example, imagine that there is an investment opportunity but you do not have the money or the capacity to access funds. The opportunity exists, but you are not prepared. It is always both.

The current scenario is complicated by runaway inflation, a real threat that erodes the purchasing power of our money. This phenomenon not only increases the cost of living significantly, but also jeopardizes our ability to save and the financial decisions we make on a daily basis. At the same time, the increase in interest rates adds an extra layer of complexity to our debt management, raising the costs associated with loans and credit, and forcing us to rethink our financial strategies.

It is imperative to diversify our sources of income and consider lifestyle adjustments to align ourselves with the new economic realities. In addition, it is essential to strengthen our debt management, looking for ways to minimize negative impacts and protect our financial well-being. However, this analysis is not only limited to identifying risks and challenges; it also offers us the opportunity to discover emerging sectors and business models that show signs of prosperity even in times of uncertainty. Remaining alert and receptive to these opportunities can be critical to successfully adapting to changing economic circumstances.

But reflection and action should not stop there. It is crucial to understand that adaptability and flexibility are indispensable qualities in this scenario. The ability to reinvent oneself, whether through learning new skills, exploring different fields of work or even considering new business ventures, becomes a valuable tool to ensure not only our survival, but also our flourishing in these challenging times.

A thorough analysis of our financial situation in the current context is not only an exercise in self-knowledge and foresight, but also a strategy for survival and success. By bravely and strategically facing the economic storm, armed with knowledge, anticipation and adaptability, we are not only safeguarding our present, but actively building a more prosperous and secure future. In these times of constant change, our resilience and ability to adapt and thrive define the path to lasting financial well-being.

Analysis of the financial situation personal

Analysis of one's personal financial situation is critical to maintaining economic stability in times of uncertainty. By evaluating income and expenses, areas for improvement can be identified and steps can be taken to ensure long-term financial sustainability. For example, by conducting a detailed analysis of monthly expenses, it is possible to identify items where spending can be reduced, such as entertainment, meals out or unnecessary subscriptions. Also, by comparing income with expenses, it can be determined whether there is a deficit or a surplus, which will allow the budget to be adjusted accordingly.

In addition, it is critical to consider the impact of debt, particularly credit card use. For example, by analyzing the outstanding balance on credit cards and the associated interest rates, you can determine if a payment plan is necessary to effectively reduce debt. Here's how to do it:

Step 1: Assess your financial situation

- Identify all your debts, including balances and interest rates.
- Calculate your monthly income and fixed expenses to see how much you can afford to spend on debt repayment.

Step 2: Prioritize your expenses

- Reduce non-essential spending to free up more funds for debt repayment.
- Adjust your monthly budget to allocate a specific amount to credit card payments.

Step 3: Create a detailed budget

- Allocate a fixed amount for the payment of credit card debt in your monthly budget.

Step 4: Free up more money

- Consider selling unwanted items or seeking additional sources of income through side jobs.

Step 5: Establish a payment strategy

- Choose a payment approach, such as the snowball method (pay off the smallest debts first) or the avalanche method (tackle the debts with the highest interest rates first).

An example of how you could structure a payment plan in a simple way using a word processor or spreadsheet. Here is an example of how you could organize the information:

Debt	Balance	Interest Rate	Minimum Payment
Credit Card A	$5,000	18%	$200
Credit Card B	$3,000	22%	$150
Personal loan	$2,000	7%	$100

In this table, you could list all of your credit card debts, including the current balance, interest rate and minimum payment required. From this information, you could develop a payment plan that allows you to prioritize the debts with the highest interest rates, or those with the lowest balances, depending on your strategy.

Refinancing options, such as debt consolidation through a personal loan with more favorable interest rates, can also be explored.

For financing I recommend using credit unions, but do not disdain banks as they have their advantages as well. As if this were a soccer team, here are the advantages of one or the other:

Advantages of credit unions:

1. Lower interest rates and fees: The cooperatives of

Savings and loan companies usually offer lower interest rates on loans and credit cards, and lower fees compared to banks.

2. Greater focus on customer service: Credit unions tend to offer more personali- zed and member-centered service, as they are run by and for their members.

3. Federal insurance: Like banks, credit unions are federally insured, which means that deposits are protected up to a certain limit.

Advantages of banks:

1. Greater availability of branches and ATMs: Banks tend to have a wider network of branches and ATMs, which can make it more convenient to access their services.

2. Greater variety of financial products: Banks generally offer a wider range of financial products and services, such as investment accounts and financial planning.

3. Increased availability of online services: Banks generally offer a wider range of online services, such as mobile banking and financial management tools.

Analysis of the personal financial situation can often result in a number of different

It's an overwhelming task, which leads to procrastination. I call it ostriching: it's sticking your head in a hole and leaving your butt out to get screwed. Doesn't that seem ridiculous? If I tell my 3-year-old daughter who is afraid of the dark that she has to face her fears, why are adults so afraid and lazy about it? I answer: because you might find something you didn't want to see.

The tables should be turned and it should be considered a game. Something worth exploring. If kept in order and approached systematically, it can be surprisingly entertaining. Financial analysis provides the basis for informed financial decisions and the implementation of concrete measures to ensure economic stability at the individual level. This process of reflection and evaluation makes it possible to determine the summary of the current financial situation, generating estimates, projections and identifying strengths and weaknesses. Through a financial study, processes can be facilitated at the time of making financial decisions, since it allows the identification of both weak and strong points, based on the data present in the financial statements.

Identification of areas and sources of income

Here is a suggested budget for beginners, designed to help you organize your finances efficiently:

- **Total Income:** Start by calculating your total after-tax income. This includes your salary, any additional income you might have, such as side jobs, bonuses, etc.

- **Fixed Expenses**: List your fixed monthly expenses. These are the payments you must make each month that generally do not change, such as rent or mortgage, student loan payments, car insurance, utility bills (if consistent), subscriptions, etc.

- **Variable Expenses**: Identify your variable expenses. These expenses can fluctuate from month to month, such as food, gas, entertainment, personal purchases, and any other non-fixed expenses.

- **Savings:** It is crucial to set aside a portion of your income for savings. A general rule of thumb is to save at least 20% of your income. You can include here your emergency fund, savings for long-term goals, investments, etc.

- **Adjustments:** If your expenses exceed your income, look for areas where you can make adjustments. This could mean reducing variable expenses or finding ways to increase your income.

- **Monthly Review:** Review your budget monthly and adjust as needed. This will help you stay on track and make proactive changes to your spending habits.

Here is a detailed breakdown of a beginner's budget with a monthly income of $3,000. This example is designed to help you organize your finances efficiently:

Category	Amount/Description
Total Revenues	$3,000 (100%)
Fixed Expenses	$1,200 (40%)
Rental	$800
Student loans	$200
Auto insurance	$100
Subscriptions (Internet, Netflix)	$100
Variable Expenses	$y00 (30%)
Food	$400
Gasoline	$150
Entertainment and personal shopping	$350
Savings	$500 (20%)
Emergency fund	$300
Vacation savings	$150
Investments	$150
Settings	$300 (10%)

This budget outline is just a starting point. Everyone has different financial needs and objectives, so it is important to tailor your budget to your particular situation. Remember to review and adjust your budget monthly to make sure it reflects your current needs and keeps you on track toward your financial goals.

Identification of areas and sources of income

In the face of the looming economic crisis, it is critical to identify additional areas and sources of income to maintain financial stability. For example, exploring independent work opportunities or side businesses can provide an additional financial cushion. As with everything in life, you have to walk with your radar on. When a specific idea comes to mind, and you see potential, you may want to test it out. For all that, I have already passed on information in previous chapters on how to treat it as a project.

In the current context, the rise of e-commerce has provided opportunities for online ventures, such as the sale of handmade products or the provision of specialized services. E-Commerce is very saturated, but there is always a way to monetize, it is just a matter of finding the opportunity.

Any other more traditional person would tell you that there are sectors that traditionally do not suffer in times of crisis. A quick Google search will give you one or another information depending on the author. What is clear to me is that nobody is going to give you the secret, because if not, they would not monetize it first.

If it is clear to us that fortunes are created in periods of crisis, and that you are not a guy with great investment capacity, like most humans, what we have to do is to be on the lookout for opportunities. Stop looking at the ground when you walk and ask around you. Opportunity is where you least expect it. These examples should be useful to give you an idea of the opportunities that are often in demand.

Category	Examples	Estimated Cash Receipts
Secondary Businesses rios (Side Hustles)	E-commerce (Dropshipping, Amazon FBA)	$200 - $5000/month* $200 - $5000/month* $200 - $5000/month* $200 - $5000/month
	Creation and sale of digital courses	$500 - $7000/month* $500 - $7000/month* $500 - $7000/month* $500 - $7000/month
	Investment in cryptocurrencies (requires knowledge)	Varies widely
Freelance Platforms Trend Jobs	Web development and mobile	$500 - $10000/ project
	Digital marketing (SEO, SEM)	$300 - $5000/ project
	UI/UX Design	$500 - $4000/ project
	Social media management	$300 - $3000/month
Opportunities without Specialized Skills	Property management on Airbnb	$500 - $10000/month* $500 - $10000/month* $500 - $10000/month* $500 - $10000/month
	Sale of stock photos	$100 - $500/month

	Dog walker or pet care	$15 - $25/hour

*These amounts are estimates and may vary depending on

multiple factors such as location, market demand, hours of work and marketing strategies employed.

Remember that success in any side hustle or freelance work depends not only on identifying a good opportunity, but also on your dedication, quality of work, marketing skills and ability to adapt to market needs. In addition, it is important to conduct research and consider the potential return on investment before committing significant resources to any new venture.

Beware of false gurus and promises of instant riches

In the digital era in which we live, promises of instant wealth and dazzling success flood every corner of our social networks, especially when it comes to digital marketing. These promises, often emanating from so-called marketing or financial "gurus," create a mirage of success that, at first glance, seems within reach. But is it really as simple as it is portrayed or is its content based on satisfying the algorithm?

Do they really think their trading coach makes a living from trading or does he or she actually make a living from coaching?

There is an uncomfortable truth that many choose to ignore: behind those courses and affiliate strategies that promise to turn you into an overnight millionaire, there is a very lucrative business...

but not precisely for those who buy these courses. Most of these figures generate their income not from applying the strategies they teach, but from selling the illusion that you can do it too, if you just buy their "secret".

There is a lot of valid and free information online. At the end of the day everyone should be concerned with planting and watering their mental garden with options, but don't become dogmatic about any one person or coach. No one is in possession of the truth or the formula for success. I recommend you do as a college professor told me a million years ago: "Plagiarizing from one source is called copying, copying from many sources is called researching. Do your research and draw your conclusions."

Forms of financing corporate

In a landscape where the American middle-class dream has disappeared and job stability is a privilege of the past, there is a pressing need for entrepreneurship. The era of working for decades for a single employer and retiring with a sense of security has come to an end. In this ever-changing context, the ability to conceive and develop one's own business becomes a crucial skill to thrive.

For both startups and established businesses, evaluating the forms of financing available is crucial to ensure viability and growth. For example, startups often rely first and foremost on using the owner's personal credit card or the closest family member who trusts your chances. Then

After a period of time and if feasible, there are rounds of seed financing or angel investors to raise the necessary capital to fuel their initial growth.

On the other hand, established companies may consider long-term financing options, such as issuing bonds or obtaining loans to finance expansion or modernization projects.

In addition, it is critical to consider the impact of the capital structure on the financial health of the company. For example, assessing the ratio of debt to equity in the financing structure can provide valuable information about the company's solvency and debt capacity. But that's too much trouble, and for that there are people whose job it is to be a CFO. If, on the other hand, you have to be everything in your company, here are the most common products when it comes to financing your company.

Also, considering the tax and financial implications of different forms of financing is crucial to making informed decisions on the optimal capital structure.

Line of credit.

A line of credit is a financial tool that allows a company to access funds on a flexible basis, up to a pre-established limit, as needed. This revolving credit facility can be obtained through banks or other financial institutions, and can be secured or unsecured. Secured lines of credit are usually backed by the company's assets.

The company's credit facilities, such as accounts receivable or inventory, may result in lower interest rates. On the other hand, unsecured lines of credit do not require collateral, but may have higher interest rates. It is important to note that lines of credit may be subject to fees and charges, and failure to comply with the terms of the agreement may result in financial penalties.

How to get it?

To obtain a line of credit, a company must submit an application to a financial institution. The application will generally require detailed information about the company, its financial statements, its credit history, and the assets to be used as collateral, if applicable. The approval of a line of credit and its terms will depend on an assessment of the company's creditworthiness and its ability to repay the credit.

Business loans.

A business loan is a form of financing that companies can obtain to cover operating expenses, expand their operations, or finance specific projects. There are different types of business loans, each with its own characteristics and requirements.

How to Get a Business Loan?

In order to obtain a business loan, companies can apply to

to different sources of financing, such as banks, financial institutions, or government programs. It is important to submit an application that includes detailed information about the company, its financial statements, credit history, and assets to be used as collateral, if applicable. The approval of the loan and its terms will depend on the evaluation of the company's creditworthiness and its ability to repay the loan.

Purchase Order (PO)

A Purchase Order is a request from a customer to purchase goods or services from a supplier. It is a legal document that details the items, quantities, agreed prices, payment terms and delivery date. To obtain financing to fulfill large orders, companies may use commercial loans or lines of credit.

Merchant Cash Advances

Merchant Cash Advances are a form of financing in which a company receives a cash advance in exchange for a portion of its future sales. This type of financing can be useful to cover immediate operating expenses or to finance marketing campaigns.

Hard Money

Hard Loans are short-term financing solutions backed by an asset, such as real estate.

ria. They are often used in real estate investment projects. Due to their higher interest rates, it is recommended to use them with caution and only for projects with a clear return potential.

Inventory Advances

Inventory Advances are loans used to finance the purchase of inventory. These loans can be useful for companies that need additional capital to purchase inventory and cover operating expenses during periods of high demand.

Factoring

Factoring is a financial transaction in which a company sells its accounts receivable to a third party at a discounted price. This form of financing can provide companies with immediate access to cash, helping them to manage cash flow and finance operations.

Business Helper Loans

Small Business Loans provide financial assistance to emerging or small businesses. These loans can range from grants to special programs for small businesses, and can be useful for financing operations, growth investments, and other business needs.

In such a changing economic environment, it is essential for both individuals and companies to be aware of the various financial products, suppliers and the advantages and disadvantages of the various financial products.

tes associated with each. It's not just a loan or a credit card, there are a multitude of options and resources that may not be ideal in some cases, but are the least expensive option than the most affordable.

The lack of generalized knowledge of personal and business finance has been identified as a determining factor in individual and corporate finances, and may be related to the lack of preparation for making informed financial decisions. Therefore, financial education has become a pillar of personal and business development, and its implementation in the educational curriculum is considered a key strategy to prevent the emergence of new economic crises.

It is important to understand that financial statements are a fundamental tool for evaluating a company's economic situation, and that the analysis and interpretation of this information is essential for understanding the company's operating behavior, identifying strengths and weaknesses, and predicting future events. In addition, knowledge of financial analysis techniques can help managers and owners evaluate the company more effectively, which in turn can improve operations and financial negotiations.

In times of crisis, whether at a personal or business level, it is essential to be aware of the sectors that are most resistant to economic fluctuations. For example, the food and beverage industry, as well as rental and retail-related businesses, tend to be more resilient in times of crisis. In addition, there are government programs and financial gimmicks that can be used to help the economy in times of crisis.

to mitigate the effects of the crisis and maintain financial stability.

In summary, knowledge of financial products, providers, financial analysis techniques, and crisis-resistant sectors, as well as access to government programs and financial tricks, are fundamental elements for making informed financial decisions and effectively managing personal and business finances in a changing economic environment.

LOVE

Section 1: Analysis

Current or past relationships, are you the problem?

You have to assume that if anyone screwed up in the first place, it's you. Don't point the finger at your spouse. I tell you this because it is better to act on oneself and make decisions from the self than to try to change or look for someone else's fault, especially that person you love.

Always start by analyzing yourself and you will surely see that you are not as perfect as you imagine. At the end of the day, and pardon the pun, we all think our own farts smell good. That's why you have to identify patterns and do an exercise of introspection.

I'm not telling you to be meditative, but to look at it from a pragmatic point of view.

Do you notice a repeating pattern in your love or family failures? Maybe the uncomfortable answer is: yes, the problem is you. But don't worry, here's how to deal with that reality.

Now take paper and pencil and make a list of your recent relationships.

significant. Write down the good, the bad, and most of all, how they ended. Do you see a pattern? For example, do you always end up arguing about the same thing? Do you feel you are not valued? This initial analysis is crucial to understand the starting point.

Once you have that list in front of you, take a moment to reflect on what you have written. Look not only for patterns in how these relationships ended, but also in how they began and developed. Ask yourself: Is there any consistent behavior on your part that may have contributed to these outcomes?
Are there any fears or insecurities? Are there specific characteristics in the people you choose that could be influencing these patterns?

Now, focusing on the present, if you are currently in a relationship, perform the same analysis. Note which aspects you consider positive and which negative. Reflect on how conflict, communication, mutual support, and overall satisfaction are handled in the relationship. Do you identify any similarities with your past relationships that may be a cause for concern or, on the contrary, do you see signs of growth and positive change in yourself?

If you have broken the cycle, congratulations, but as we already know that the goat always pulls for the hill, you have to watch out for inherent and impulsive behaviors and sometimes, why not, re-educate yourself and bite your tongue.

To do this exercise I put a table below, but I want you to keep in mind that you should not do this to judge yourself or to blame others, but to give you a clearer perspective of your relational patterns.

With this understanding, you can begin to work on specific areas of improvement, both in yourself and in your current or future relationships. For example, if you notice that you tend to avoid conflict, you might work on developing assertive communication skills. Or if you find that you frequently feel unappreciated, it might be helpful to reflect on your boundaries and how to communicate effectively. Remember, the goal of this exercise is to foster personal growth that leads to healthier and more satisfying relationships. Introspection is the first step toward change and sometimes it hurts too much but it is necessary. As you move forward, be gentle with yourself and understanding but don't sabotage yourself with excessive self-justification to protect your ego, be consistent and accept the screw-ups. Change takes time, and every step, no matter how small, is progress toward a fuller and happier life in the realm of personal relationships.

Here are the questions:

Ask	Reflection Objective
What positive aspects would I highlight from my past relationships?	Identify what you value and you want in a relationship.
What negative aspects are repeated in my relationships?	Recognize problem patterns that may need attention.
How have I handled conflicts in my relationships?	Assess your ability to resolve disagreements in a healthy way.

Do I feel valued and understood in my relationships? Why yes or why no?	Reflect on reciprocity and recognition in your relationships.
Have I noticed any trends in the type of person I choose to establish a relationship with?	Identify if there are specific characteristics in the people you are attracted to or looking for.
How did my previous relationships end and what did I learn from each ending?	To learn lessons from past experiences to apply in the future.
In my current relationship (if applicable), What do I value most and what would I like to improve?	Reflect on the current state of your relationship and areas for growth.
What am I doing differently in my current relationship compared to the past?	Recognize changes and improvements in your behavior or approach to relationships.
How do I react to criticism or problems within my relationship?	Evaluate your receptivity and ability to work on negative feedback.
What am I willing to change or improve in myself to nurture my relationships?	Commitment to personal growth for healthier relationships.

Identify Patterns or Traumas

Now that you have your list, it's time to go even deeper. Many times, our patterns in relationships are echoes of past experiences, even from childhood. To confront these patterns, you must first acknowledge and accept them. It is not easy, but it is the first step to change. And I repeat again for the sake of clarity: it is important not to fall into self-pity or self-incriticism.

mination. It is not about blaming yourself, but about understanding and learning. For example, if you find that you tend to choose partners who do not value you, ask yourself: What personal beliefs or experiences are influencing this choice? How can you change it?

The key here is active introspection. It is not enough to acknowledge the problem; you need to actively work to change it. This could include reading books on personal development, attending workshops, or even seeking therapy. Books like this go only so far, if you think it's repetitive and you can't fix it yourself, it's critical to seek out someone professional.

I do not intend to fall into the cliché of telling you what to do because I am not a psychologist, but you have to be aware of when you have a problem and act to fix it. But please, don't become one of those ridiculous do-gooders who go around giving thanks to vibes and colored stones. To each one what works for him, but if you are into that kind of stuff and you think it works for you, then you should definitely see a psychologist.

Section 2: Resources

Professional advice

As you know, in this book I am not going to dogmatize with ridiculous theories and methods invented by new age philosophy and four badly rolled joints.

If you sprain your ankle, you go to the doctor. If you get the flu, you go to the doctor.

If you have an accident, the doctor comes to you. The same with the head.

If something is wrong, you go to the doctor.

Enough with the stigma of psychologists. If there is something wrong with your head, you go to a professional for advice and besides, it is quite likely that over the years the pieces will fall out of our heads and we will be missing some screws caused by traumas and problems. As the famous sticker says: Shit Happens.

Seeing a psychologist is a valuable tool for improving personal relationships. A good counselor can help you understand your own thoughts and emotions, as well as find solutions to problems you may be facing.

Here is detailed information on how to find the right consultant for you:

Identify what's on your mind: First things first, you need to know what's bothering you: Relationship problems? Family feuds? Or is it personal demons like anxiety or depression? Knowing what's biting you will help you find the right specialist.

Do your research, but don't go crazy: There are as many therapeutic approaches as there are fish in the sea. From cognitive behavioral therapy that helps you change your toxic thoughts, to systemic therapy that sees your family drama as a soap opera episode. Take a look at Google, but don't drown in information. Pick the one that resonates with you and go for it.

Ask questions, make inquiries, seek references: If you know someone who has gotten out of the hole with professional help, ask them for recommendations.

nes. You can also search for reviews online. The experiences of others can be beacons in your search.

Test the water before you jump in: Before committing to a therapy marathon, schedule a first appointment. It's your chance to test the waters and see if there's chemistry with the therapist. The connection with the one who will untangle your brain is vital.

Commit yourself, but really: Therapy is not instant magic. It requires your time, your effort and, above all, your patience. Change comes with commitment and collaboration, not by magic.

AND VERY IMPORTANT:

AVOID PSEUDO GURUS, RIDICULOUS INSTAGRAMMERS AND
NEW AGE, NEW AGE TECHNIQUES, SMART MOMS, NEW AGE TECHNIQUES
FASHION, MOTIVATIONAL COACHES, and other charlatans who have NO FUCKING IDEA what they are talking about and only create content to give you endorphins and take your money. Don't let yourself be fooled by goody two shoes.

Section 3: Practical

Here are a few situations that we often have to deal with as a couple and tactics that are often proposed.

How to talk and discuss without ending up shouting

Let's get to the point, because the field is already full of flowers. Communication is the soul of any relationship, even if sometimes it's too hard to talk and at other times it's best to shut up, walk away and come back with a cool head (sound familiar?). So, here are a few tricks so you don't end up making the drama of the century every time you try to speak your mind.

Listen as if your life depended on it: Active listening is not just letting the other person's mouth move while you plan your next move. It is giving them your full attention, with all your senses. Watch how he moves his hands, the tone of voice he uses, and even that vein in his forehead that swells when he's about to drop the bomb. Ask questions that show you're really there, not just present. You'll show respect and, who knows, even learn something new. Do neperian logarithms, advanced logic or HTML programming if you have to, but solve what's in front of you by speaking coherently.

Speak from the heart, not with an accusing finger: Instead of hurling accusations like there's no tomorrow, start your sentences with "I feel...". Change the "You're a mess" to "I feel frustrated when I see the room turned upside down". You'll see how the shield comes down and the dialogue opens up. You know your partner better than anyone, you know which buttons you can and can't touch to move between screens in the video game.

Take a breath before releasing the pump: If you feel the boiler is about to explode, put the meter on pause. Breathe

count to ten (or a hundred, if necessary). Think about what you really want to say and how to say it without sounding like the start of World War III. If not, keep it to yourself, and there will be a time to talk about it when the waters are calmer. Ask for time politely and come back to it calmly.

Learn to dance with your anger: Anger is like that pain in the ass: it's there, and you have to deal with it. Recognize when the ego starts to take over and find a way to express it without it becoming a flamethrower. Talking about your feelings calmly can be more therapeutic than you think, even if it feels like you're going to break out in rashes from anger.

The body also speaks: It's not all what you say, but how you say it. Your posture, your gestures, and even your tone of voice sing the Traviata before you know it. Keep an open attitude, one that invites small talk, not mourning. And if you're lucky, and you fix it, get laid post-fight.

Examples of real-life cases

Let's break down how these communication tricks can be applied in the most common battlegrounds: couple, family, and work. Because, let's face it, sometimes it feels like we need an instruction manual to handle these arenas.

Couple case: weekend plans in dispute

Imagine that you want to spend the weekend lying on the couch watching marathons of series, but your partner dreams of a getaway.

romantic to the field. Instead of turning it into the argument of the next world war, use active listening. Let your partner state his or her reasons with passion, observe his or her gestures, those that say more than a thousand words. Then, with your heart in your hand, express your wishes. "I feel exhausted this week and I was dreaming of resting at home". Find that middle ground where you can both give in a little without feeling like you're losing the battle. Maybe a day in the field and a day on the couch is the peace treaty you need.

Family case: the eternal drama of who does what

Who should take out the garbage or who hasn't washed the dishes in days?
Discussions about parenting? Before the house becomes a battlefield, invite a round table discussion. Listen to each family warrior: what do they propose? How do they feel? Then, as an ambassador of peace (if necessary, dress up as Pope Pius XII), come up with a solution where everyone does their bit. Perhaps a calendar of tasks will be the protective shield that will prevent future conflicts.

Case Labor: navigating the sea of labor relations

Have you ever tried to assemble a piece of Ikea furniture without instructions? Surely when doing it you have forgotten some step and you have had to disassemble it because you forgot a small screw. Well, even the smallest detail matters and it is very important to keep the forms and follow established guidelines. When the time comes to give feedback to that colleague who is always late with his reports, do it tactfully. "I have noticed that the last few reports

I'm concerned about how this is affecting the team. Offer help, look for solutions together instead of dropping the problem like a bomb. In meetings, practice active listening and foster an environment where everyone feels comfortable expressing their ideas. Diplomacy should be your best ally in the corporate jungle. And please don't be the passive-aggressive office jerk.

In each of these scenarios, remember that the goal is not to win the argument, but to find a solution that benefits everyone involved. You learn that lesson as you get older. It doesn't matter that you win in the moment, but that you gain peace of mind in the long run. The difference between winning the battle and winning the war. In the end, what we all want is peace of mind and assets. Effective communication is your best tool for building bridges and keeping fires at bay, whether at home, in love or at the office. Put these strategies into practice and you will see how even the most tense situations can be transformed into opportunities to strengthen your relationships and, in the process, become a responsible and trustworthy leader. In the end, it's all advantages.

Children. Enjoy and at the same time educate

I have a serious problem with Instamoms. It makes me very volatile to have a hippie vegan tell me ridiculous methods without even having a degree. It's clear that to be a parent you have to learn. What's more, many are parents and shouldn't be, but that topic is best left unaddressed here.

Here I am going to give you from a more empirical point of view how I think you should organize your time with the children and enjoy it. There is one way: structure and order. Children like to compartmentalize the day, have clear instructions and probably like to challenge you to show their own judgment.

Even at the risk of sounding like one of those I mentioned earlier, enjoying children and raising them simultaneously is an art that requires patience, dedication and, above all, love. Faced with an avalanche of ridiculous advice on all sides, it's easy to feel overwhelmed and skeptical. However, beyond academic credentials or lack thereof (the neighbor on the fifth floor, the fishmonger or the mother-in-law), what really matters is finding an approach that works for you and your children.

The structure and the order.

Children thrive in predictable environments where they know what to expect and what is expected of them. This does not mean extreme rigidity, but establishing a daily routine that balances educational activities, free play, and family time. In my case it is sometimes difficult to maintain that structure since there is always an opportunity to skip it, but if done judiciously, it can even help us adults maintain order in our other pursuits. For example, if your kids go to bed at an early hour, don't be silly and go to bed after watching 3 episodes of the new Netflix series in a row. If the kids have to eat a balanced meal, take advantage of it and eat what they eat, not their candy bars.

Here are some practical suggestions to organize your time with the kids and enjoy the process:

Establish daily routines: Routines provide security and stability. From wake-up time to bedtime, mealtimes, study time and playtime, a clear structure helps children feel secure and know what comes next. If the child knows the exact order of activities (as they do at school or daycare), it's easier for them to follow your lead and you avoid problems because there is an expectation. Creating a daily structure does not mean setting rules for every second and minute of the day or making Excel charts, but rather providing them with a safe and predictable framework within which they can explore, learn and, of course, play. Children thrive on routine because it gives them security and teaches them to manage their own expectations and those of the world around them.

Involve them in planning: Although you set the ground rules, involving your children in planning some activities gives them a sense of autonomy and motivates them to participate more actively. This can include choosing which books to read together or deciding which family games to play. The important thing is to make them feel involved in decision making and encourage their inner leadership.

Clear instructions and realistic expectations: By setting clear instructions, you facilitate their understanding of what is expected of them, which is crucial for their development. This not only helps them develop a sense of responsibility, but also allows them to exercise their autonomy within safe boundaries. Allowing them to challenge you by showing their own judgment is, in fact, an excellent way to help them develop a sense of responsibility.

This is a great way to encourage their critical thinking and their ability to make decisions, but be careful, as it can become a double-edged sword and they may become a protestor. It is necessary to set limits and let him understand that he is listened to and valued, but not spoiled.

Quality vs. quantity time: This is more for parents than for children. I will give you a personal example: I often felt guilty because I always have it in my head that time will never come back. I know that someday, when my daughters are older, I'm looking forward to going back to the current time of 5 and 3 years old. But now, there are also times when I am wishing I had my time alone or with my wife or when I am with them there is no quality time. It's not about spending all day together, it's about making the moments together count. Even on a busy afternoon, 15 minutes of uninterrupted play or conversation can make a big difference to them and to you.

Learning through play: Play is a powerful tool for learning. Through play, children explore the world, develop social and cognitive skills, and learn to solve problems. Choose games and activities that stimulate their curiosity and teach them new concepts in a fun way; play with them, and let them play on their own. It is clear to us that we must encourage their imagination in their play and let them do it on their own.

Encourage independence: As your children get older, it is important to give them small responsibilities that they can handle. This helps them develop self-confidence and understand the value of work and effort. It is very satisfying to see how proud they feel when they help you cook or clean something. Just like an adult, they also want to feel useful, so giving them small responsibilities will not only help you, but will also help build their character. The point is not only to have them learn to pick up their toys without protest or put their plate in the sink, but maybe start with something more engaging and build from there.

Be a role model: As an adult, your behavior is a role model. Showing them how to manage time, how to deal with challenges and how to balance work and play is as important as any direct lesson you can teach them. Being aware of this and acting on it can be one of the most meaningful gifts you give your children. Children learn by imitating.

Adapt and learn: Every child is unique, and what works for one may not work for another. That was hard for me to understand at first. You have to be open to adapt your approach and learn from the experience.

Dedicate time, dedication and effort

And here, in the final stretch, let's dive right into that topic that many avoid as if it were a Christmas diet: effort and dedication in your relationships, both at home and at work.

Prioritization

This is something that sounds like a Sunday afternoon chore, but it's crucial. Between that series marathon and your endless scrolling on your cell phone, you already have enough tools to think about what really matters to you. Family? Work? The project of raising iguanas on your balcony? Whatever it is, start living your life with a clear purpose and put limits on everything else so it doesn't eat up your time like there's no tomorrow. Balance, that's the key.

Plan quality time

Here's the juicy part: scheduling those moments that make it all worthwhile. I'm not talking about sending a WhatsApp while zapping, but planning family dinners where cell phones are forbidden, getaways with your partner that don't involve standing in line at the supermarket, or evenings with friends where the only plan is to laugh until your stomach hurts. It's those moments that recharge your batteries and remind you why you got into this mess of human relationships. If you don't plan for the basics, you're leaving eventualities, and believe me, problems, to chance.

Self-care

If you are not well, nothing can be well. Yes, it sounds like a spa slogan, but it's the truth. If you're a mess, how are you going to be there for others? Find time to sweat it out at the gym, meditate, or just lay on the couch and do absolutely nothing.

Those "me to me" moments are sacred.

and necessary for you to be able to give the best version of yourself to those you meet.

surround.

So you know, putting your heart into your relationship involves much more than just sending a heart emoji from time to time. It requires dedication, effort, and yes, sometimes sacrificing a little of that precious "I" for the "we".

Section 4: Some Tips

Relationships are not always an easy road, but with a little attention we can avoid many potholes. In my opinion there are 3 fundamental points where the balloon can burst. So to speak, there are 3 places where our defense is more exposed and sometimes we are not even aware of it. That is why it is essential to take this into account in order to act accordingly.

Impact of Social Networks

It is clear that social networking has reshaped our interactions to an extent unrecognizable from just a few decades ago. I dread to think how my daughters will acquire the social skills necessary to be fully socially adjusted individuals. On the other hand, I am also concerned about how the new generations will approach the issue. In my opinion, the pandemic was a turning point where we were forced to be completely isolated and 100% dependent on that remote feeling. Young people were flirting using Tinder instead of going to a bar and talking nonsense, and instead of going to the supermarket, they were bringing it home to you. You have to have

Keep in mind that social networks are only one player in this game and be very clear that they are private, for-profit companies. They are not there to help you, but to capture your attention and keep you glued to the screen as long as possible in order to monetize your impressions into money. They don't care about your political ideals or your life as a couple; what they want is to find out what you like and give you three more cups of it. What do you like about chocolate? Take three cups. What do you like about animal posts? Take zoos, kittens, environmentalists, etc. All of this, as you know, has contributed to the separation of ideals in society, to conflict and to the thought that we are more ideologically separated than ever. And the fact is that, basically, with social networks, any asshole has a voice, and that is a problem.

As for personal relationships, if you are one of those who after a day of hard work come home to sit on the couch to watch TV next to your partner and in the meantime you are sending memes to each other, you have a problem. TALK. Facebook, Instagram, X, they all promise to bring us closer, but at what cost? The key is not to let these platforms dictate how we feel about our relationships. To mitigate their impact, I suggest a weekly digital detox. This involves selecting one day a week where you voluntarily reduce the use of social networks to the essential minimum. You can activate the 'screen time', leave it on the landing as soon as you enter the house or on top of a very high cabinet. During this time, focus on activities that strengthen your direct relationships: a meal, a family game afternoon or simply a face-to-face conversation with your partner without screens in between. Humans need humanity.

Conflict Management

Conflicts are inevitable, but their effective resolution is an art that can be learned. It is often difficult to balance ego with existing problems, so one of the most effective methods is the "I-message" technique. This technique involves expressing your feelings from a personal perspective without assigning blame. For example, instead of saying, "You make me feel ignored," you can say, "I feel ignored when I look around and see that everyone is on their phone. Yes, I know you're thinking that at the critical moment of being on edge and arguing you're going to be thinking about grammar and neperian logarithms, but as they say in my village: "A joderse y aguantarse".

This small change in language invites reflection rather than defensiveness, opening the space for constructive dialogue. Also, establish a "pause code" in heated discussions. If you feel tension rising, agree with your partner or friend to take a brief pause to breathe and calm down before continuing the conversation. It also helps to have a "safe" word so you can come back to it when the dust settles, as often as necessary. But just talk it out, don't swallow it or shy away from conflict. I think I've already said it, but I'll say it again: if the shit gets covered up, it still smells. So it's important to talk things out like adults and that contributes to a transparent and healthy relationship.

Focus on Self-Esteem

The way we perceive ourselves plays a determining role in how we interact with others. Strong self-esteem allows us to face challenges and offer emotional support when needed. Plus, I don't know exactly why, but we even look better looking (it must be the energy that comes off).

At this point in the book I have given you a multitude of techniques to reach this point with certain guarantees.

Remember, loving yourself is not an act of selfishness; it is the basis for loving others in a healthy and balanced way. Think of it as filling your glass until it overflows; only then can you begin to fill the glasses of others without running dry. Be water my friend. So, give yourself permission to put yourself first once in a while. By doing so, you are not only doing yourself a favor, but also the people around you.

EPILOGUE

And so, after unraveling a plan of action, we come to the end of this journey. I do not pretend that now when you implement everything will be a bed of roses with sugary tips and pats on the back. There will probably be times that are boring and demotivating, but you have to have faith that there is always a way out of the tunnel at the end. The only thing I intend here is to show you the way, the rest, you have to walk and be constant.

But do not take it to the tremendous, if you are over 40, as in my case, you must think that you are winning the game, and now in this second part you have to keep and play counterattack. It's going to be a tough journey until you get used to it, but if you've made it this far, we can say that we're going to walk it together. Step by step, we are walking.

I have sought to share with you not magic recipes or hidden secrets of the ancient sages, but a sincere and practical perspective from someone who, like you, is in the daily struggle to improve, to be a better parent, a better professional, and above all, a better person. This book is a reflection of my commitment not only to you, the reader, but also to myself. A commitment to honesty, not to sell you smoke and mirrors.

Throughout these pages, I hope to have provided you with more than just advice: a vision, a mirror in which you may have seen yourself reflected on more than one occasion, and above all, a push to take action. Because at the end of the day, the only thing that differentiates those who achieve their goals from those who fall by the wayside is action. The ability to get up every morning with the determination to face whatever comes, to learn from failures, to never give up and always keep walking without stopping.

I want you to know that you are not alone in this journey. We all have our bad days, our failures and our insecurities. But we also have the ability to overcome, to learn and to move forward, stronger and wiser. You don't need to be a superhero or have a life story worthy of a movie to make significant changes in your life. You just need to have the courage to take the first step, and then the next, and so on.

Remember: the line in the sand is drawn. On one side, comfort and inaction; on the other, effort, discipline and the possibility of a full and satisfying life. Whether and how you cross that line is ultimately up to you.

So here I say goodbye, not as a guru or as an expert, but as a fellow traveler. I am on your team because I have had to reinvent myself as well. I hope this book has been a source of inspiration for you and, why not, a good companion in moments of doubt. Don't forget that real change starts with a small step, and that step is yours. But where that change is truly appreciated is in the constancy. When you know where you want to go and you make that decision, walk without stopping.

www.ingramcontent.com/pod-product-compliance
Lightning Source LLC
Chambersburg PA
CBHW071504220526
45472CB00003B/915